Secret Genealogy

by

Suellen Ocean

Secret Genealogy

by
Suellen Ocean

Published by:
Ocean-Hose
P.O. Box 115
Grass Valley, CA 95945

www.oceanhose.com
oceanhose@pacific.net

ISBN: 978-0-9651140-8-0

I wish to thank my father-in-law, Eddy Hose, for his knowledge and enthusiasm regarding the subject of Crypto-Jews. I would like to thank my mother-in-law, Dmumit Hose, for showing her Gentile daughter-in-law the beauty of Jewish heritage.

Thanks go to my son, Shane Avansino, who loves the ancient mysteries. His skill at recognizing secret society clues is amazing and his humor and knowledge made him the perfect companion while traveling in Europe and the Middle East.

I also wish to humbly thank all the genealogical researchers who over the years have shared their findings. All the cousins who, like me, love and care about our ancestors. I am grateful for the work done by Fauna Mihalko. Though she is gone, her work lives on. How kind of her to go beyond her own family tree to help others connect with their ancestors. Fauna's mention of my great-grandfather led to an immediate connection with a centuries-deep family tree.

My gratitude also goes out to the Nevada County Library where I found an abundance of quality reference material and to the librarians who extended my book loans on many occasions and guided me in the direction I needed to go.

And of course, I must thank my husband Jon. I appreciate his continued patience with my writing and publishing endeavors and his intelligent answers to my endless questions on many topics. His faith in me was what really kept me going. This was a difficult topic and he kept me grounded.

In 2002 Suellen Ocean and her husband Jon rented a motorcycle in London and rode it for a week throughout the English countryside. It was on this first European vacation that she connected to her ancestral roots across the seas. She has since returned twice to Europe and the Middle East. *Secret Genealogy* is a companion to her novel, *The Lies of the Lion*. Happily married for thirty years, she has two grown sons and three grandchildren.

"Biblical name?"

"Hebrew," she said.

"Jewish?" I asked.

"No," she said.

"Were you raised Catholic?" I asked.

"No, my mother was a rebel."

If you are not familiar with any of the words in the book, please take advantage of the glossary in the back. It will make your reading much more enjoyable.

Table of Contents

"The city of Amsterdam has long had a special relationship with the Jews. Since the end of the sixteenth century, when Jews first came there from Spain and Portugal, they and other groups had found an atmosphere of religious tolerance and political security. Amsterdam has always had a tradition of respect for diversity, for individuality, for the right of people to think and do as they please. And, therefore, this city evokes a special intimacy and affection in Jewish hearts."

Abba Eban HERITAGE –
Civilization and the Jews

Chapter One
Why Search? What Does it Mean to be Jewish?

After spending years on the genealogical websites, I have come to believe that I can help millions of Americans who have reached dead ends in regards to their family trees. Even after several years of *hunches* that my ancestors were Jewish, there was always doubt, but the ancestors cheered me on. They left proud symbols, whether it was the lions that lay crumbling to entrances of long forgotten homesteads or names they picked for their children, Rachel, Jacob, Samuel, Ezekiah. They had hope for a future where descendants were sensitive to the echo of their voices. The dead *can* talk and they knew how to leave clues, we just don't know how to look for them.

One can only imagine the conversation our ancestors had when they made a pact to *not tell the next generation they were Jewish.* For a people so proud of their heritage, it must have been for the family's survival and/or the opportunity to live *free of persecution* that this decision was arrived upon. The guilt and sadness that would have presided over the loss of such a beloved and ancient culture must have been immense.

One day while I was writing this, a man walked into the Holocaust museum in Washington and shot the bodyguard and himself. Early reports said he was linked to a *white supremacist* website. My hope is that people with lost tribal roots will find unity and love for others if those roots are found.

There are two groups of Jews that I will be referring to, the Ashkenazim and the Sephardim. Ashkenazi Jews descend from Middle, Northern and Eastern Europe and may speak *Yiddish*. The Sephardim are the descendants of Jews from Spain and Portugal and they may speak *Ladino*. Sometimes I use the expression "Hebrew" because during the Middle Ages Jews were often referred to as "Hebraic", as in the end of the 1600s, when "The Holy Office at Cartagena de Indias", denounced people for being "of the hebraic nation."

What does it mean to be Jewish? I think if you asked that question to the Jewish community you would find many answers, just as you would if you asked what is it like to be a Muslim, Buddhist, Christian or even what it means to be a mother or father or a brother or sister. Everyone has different needs and desires. I'm not Jewish and if I was born from a Jewish mother and father but did not go to Synagogue, some Jews would say I'm not Jewish. Orthodox Jews may fail to recognize the new "Reformed" Jews who have taken a modern approach to worship, bringing jazz musicians into the Shabbat service, and having an orator speak in

English instead of Hebrew. Having some Jewish ancestors does not make me Jewish. I would only be Jewish if my mother was a Jew. However, I've seen a posting on a Jewish message board where someone was not a practicing Jew but was told that if their parents/grandparents were Jews, then they had *been Jewish all along.* I'm sure you will find someone to totally disagree with that.

I love to uncover and rediscover what was lost. Too many Americans want their ancestral history to be right out of the pages of a European fairy tale. No matter how hard you try, you can't reinvent it. Our ancestors are who they were, not who we wish them to be. My ideas may require a *change in thinking* but a fascinating change, once you educate yourself on the beautiful history left behind by the Jewish people.

Let me state a couple of historical points that one should bear in mind when researching a Christian family tree. One, a Jew could convert or be forced to convert and later become a priest. Two, A Jew who converted or whose family earlier converted could become a part of Christian European society, or marry into, and obtain titles such as knight, duke, king, princess, duchess, etc. Being "Jewish" or being "Royal" is not exclusive of one another. There was Jewish royalty as well, e.g.: Hasmonean Royalty. Someone could also have had a Jewish mother and wound up in a

3

European Royal family tree. Jews were not aliens from another planet; their culture may have been different but quite often very much like others.

There is an ancient designation between the Northern Kingdom of Israel (Samaria) and the Southern Kingdom of Judah (Judea). Technically, "Jews" are the names of the descendants of Judea but "Jews" is also used when speaking of "Israelites". The twelve tribes of Israel are all the descendants of "Jacob", whose name later became "Israel". Don't feel bad if this is confusing. One of the reasons I wrote this book was so that I can return to it as a reference. There is a lot to remember and I hope to keep this as simply as I can. I will probably make the mistake of referring to the lost tribes of Israel as Jews. Although it is not technically accurate, I do it for the sake of genealogy and wanting to trace back into antiquities. It's a complicated process.

Once you find your Israelite ancestors, you can further your research and try to decipher whether they were Jews or Samarians but they were both Israelites and descended from Jacob who was referred to as a *Lion* in the Book of Genesis in the Torah/Bible. *The lion became the symbol of the Israelite tribe of Judah.*

A company called Mazornet, dedicated to compiling information and resources about Jewish genetic diseases, states that "because of wars, occupation and dispersal, most modern-day Jews are descended from the tribes of Benjamin and Judah (hence, Jews). There is, however, valid historical evidence that remnants of other tribes merged with Benjamin and Judah. Thus, most Jews today carry the blood of all the tribes of Israel."

The Ancient Hebrews were very religious. If they hadn't been, they would have been ostracized from their community. The purpose of this book is not about converting to Judaism. My intention is to guide you toward sources that will enable you to discover whether or not your ancestors were Jewish.

Though intermarrying happened within all ethnic groups, tribes, etc. the Jews of the Middle Ages did not approve of it. They were very strict with their laws and customs and they did not think it enough to have faith in God but believed it crucially important to follow the *Law of Moses*. You can see how difficult a task that must have been when being up-rooted or forced to hide. Unable to openly teach religion, at times Jewish children grew up not knowing how to practice it. The old adage, use it or lose it, rang just as true during the Middle Ages for religion as it does today for any number of disciplines. What did happen though, when they had an opportunity to regroup, was that *they tried their best to return to the old ways and the customs of the ancients.*

Please remember, if and when you are quite certain your ancestors were Jewish, you probably would not be considered Jewish unless you studied the religion and went through a rigorous succession of lessons. One does not say, "Oh, I'm three-quarters Jewish and one-quarter Native American". It would be correct though to say, "I'm one-quarter Native American and my other ancestors were Jewish".

If it hadn't been necessary for our ancestors to keep quiet about their Jewish origins, there would be no need for me to write this book. I've strived to be accurate and unbiased but I'm sure that I'm not. But I have had a lot of fun over the last few years searching for the clues to my Jewish ancestry. It's been a treasure hunt scouring four-hundred-year-old family trees and history books looking for clues.

Of utmost importance to the ancient Hebrews was the strict record keeping of descendants. Through the ages, in order to survive and prosper in dangerous environments that expelled, exterminated and imposed exorbitant taxes and fees on Jews in Europe and again in the New World, some Jewish families felt it necessary to disguise their ethnicity. When Jews came from

6

European seaports to the New World, they had a desire to be treated equally and wanted the same opportunities available to all immigrants. Many Jews who immigrated to New World settlements along the Atlantic Coastline not only kept quiet about their origins but altered their names as well. I've also come to believe that some Jewish eastern seaboard colonists who migrated west in "groups", did so with others who held Jewish ancestry, preferring to marry within the Jewish community or at least try to maintain a semblance of the *old brotherhood* pact.

One characteristic of Jewish history that will keep you engaged in this treasure hunt is that ancient brotherhood pact. There were Jews who stuck together. This one element stunned me the most. It wasn't so much the hints of Judaism in the names of my ancestors that made me continue looking for concrete evidence; it was the names of their associates. Several of the folks with whom they did business with, intermarried with, packed up wagons with and headed out into dangerous new untamed territories had Jewish names. I began using the Internet search engines to research the surnames of these "associates", putting "Jewish" before the last name. Most of these surnames had plenty of Jews with that name, you could tell by the hits that came up. They were prominent Rabbis or involved in a Jewish hospital or Synagogue or any hundreds or thousands of occupations and endeavors. It became a fun obsession. I had uncovered a conspiracy in my own family and I could not stop trying to prove it. Besides, I'm sure I'm not the only one to notice such a striking similarity between the attire of the Amish and New York's Orthodox Jews. It would not surprise me to find that Jacob Ammann (the Swiss Mennonite, who in 1620 began the sect of Mennonites now called Amish) had Jewish ancestors. There are many Jews with the South or Swiss German surname "Ammann" that means "administrator" or "tax farmer".

Searching for ancestral clues has been an adventure but not without difficulties. Not everyone "cares" about family origins. Many are as adamant about "not searching" as those are about "finding". I have often questioned my own motives. My mother had never once said she had Jewish ancestors, probably because no one had ever told her. Her great-grandmother's name was Rachel, a common name for early American women, yet I'm inclined to believe that these *Old Testament* names were a carry over from when many grandparents and great-grandparents were Jewish. I often hear, "It was very common for Colonial American Christians to have Old Testament names, that doesn't mean they were Jewish". No, it doesn't and I believed that, at first, but now that I know their story, I believe that many of these Biblical names are remnants of our ancient Jewish ancestry. Not all, but many. I have come to believe that there were many more Jewish immigrants that came to the New World than what history has recorded.

This book is not simple. It is a complicated subject and finding information about people who died hundreds of years ago is almost impossible, except for that wonderful new technology, the Internet. I have spent several years reading stranger's family trees, doctoral papers, excerpts from books, religious websites, etc. and have had the opportunity to have my library provide me with books I found referenced online. I want to share this abundance of information with you but in the most simplified manner I can.

In the beginning, there were desert people who recorded their genealogy. Sometimes they were the persecutors and at other times, they were persecuted. During their persecuted years, they were constantly being driven out of or migrating away from their homes. Early on, they went to eastern countries near their original homeland but some reports have the Jews going up to the lands now claimed by Britain. What is distinctive about the Jews is that they maintained strong ties with other Jews and endured through very difficult times. They obviously were a proud and stubborn group of folks and it was no doubt irritating to various factions yet this tenacity has saved a unique culture and left much of it intact and thriving. Even if you can't prove your suspicions of Jewish ancestry, look at the bible as not just a religious book but also a book chronicling origins through two tumultuous millenniums.

Anthropologists have found ancient Judaic artifacts and oral histories throughout the world, including Japan, India, Afghanistan, Italy, Malta, Pakistan, Germany, The Netherlands, Iran, Iraq, Africa, China, Russia, the British Isles, the list goes on. Persecution of European Jews led to New World immigration, especially due to Spain's *Inquisitional* period, when hundreds of thousands of Jews that had been living in Spain were driven out or burned at the stake. Many immigrated to Portugal where they met the same fate as in the mass conversion where the Inquisition pushed thousands of Jews into a stadium and sprinkled them with holy water. It was not a pleasant time. Many converted and pretended to be *practicing Catholics* but the authorities knew better and kept after them. In Spain and Portugal particularly, *the Crown did not want Judaism to spread*, they wanted Christianity and they resorted to some real ugly business. So the Jews hid. They hid behind religion, they cleverly changed their names and they also fled but they knew well enough to keep quiet about their Jewish origins. It must have made them very angry, of course. How do you maintain a secret identity, one that if discovered could mean your life and the life of your loved ones? The clues are hidden in their names and it is up to us to be open-minded (and brave, it's easy to look foolish) and see if we don't descend from these *Hidden Hebrews.*

For years, I've heard that Jews were a minority in America. I disagree and for the sake of technicalities, I'm going to have to set aside the myriad meanings of "Jewish". We will brush those arguments aside while we continue with our genealogical search. If you have hit a genealogical brick wall and I have lured you in, you are not "Jewish". For lack of any other way of spelling it out to you, I will continue to use the term "Jewish" to define these particular ancestors. I do find it annoying that one can share ancestry discussions with friends and say, "I'm Irish, Japanese, Scotttish, African, Arabic, French, Native American, etc." but can not say "Jewish" because of the technicalities of that expression. I must be content to say, "My ancestors were Jewish" or "I have Jewish ancestry".

I have spent years studying my own genealogy. I found, by accident, my surname among Jewish genealogical records only because I was tracing Jewish genealogy for someone else. I like to do that. I don't know what it is about genealogists, but we're a nice lot. See for yourself. You'll find genealogists with websites that reference hundreds of names. They understand that we are all connected. These big family trees, these webs of life, are all over the Internet and each day the trees grow larger. The longer you wait, the more likely it will be that you can place your ancestors into someone's family line. Unfortunately, many have hit a brick wall and are having an impossible time tracing their roots. That's where I come in. I want to help.

My mother was a Lutheran and my father was what I like to call a "Bed Baptist" because on Sunday morning he stayed in bed while we went to church. When he first met my mother, he was a Southern boy who loved to go to "Revivals". It wasn't quite my mother's style and California was not a hot spot for Revivals. My father's religious culture would have faded away if not for his endless narrations. I grew up hearing stories about the South, New Orleans in particular, and can still picture what it must have been like to witness people with long, flowing, white garments walking into marshy, southern waters to be baptized. I can still hear the old songs he sang to me to help understand his culture, spiritual songs, songs African Americans also sang and still sing today. My father was deeply religious and soulful. He believed. You could see it in his face. You could feel it when he spoke of it. He lived it.

My father, perhaps only once, mentioned that he felt our last name was originally Rotenberg, but that the "berg" had been dropped. As a child that meant nothing to me, nor did it mean anything to me as an adult until I started researching genealogy. One day, while searching for my husband's ancestors, I wound up on the Jewish message board at www.genealogy.com. It was interesting to read other's queries. From the Jewish message board I learned of the website www.sephardim.com and was thrilled to go to the name listings and find my husband's family name. It was a great day to find such an informative site and very eye opening to see all the other ancient Sephardic Jewish names. Out of habit I looked for my maiden name and there were two listings: Rotin and Rotenberg. What's interesting is that it was always right in front of me and I never saw it. *I was so conditioned to being a Christian* that it never once occurred to me that my ancestry may have been Jewish. I was always confused about why Christians studied maps of the Holy Land. It isn't just because Jesus is from Nazareth. The earliest Christians were Jewish and centuries later many of the transcribers of the Bible were Jewish.

Shortly after I discovered Sephardim.com, I found some notes I had jotted down during one of many conversations with my mother. When "googled" her ancestors, a pattern emerged. I was able to hit the ground running, because I had one strong name that led me to others in the family tree.

I love history and to me, who my ancestors were and from where they originated is fascinating. I would have lost the passion if my trails were dead-ends but that was not the case. There was always another clue, one after the other.

I've followed many trails for friends and their names clearly are not Jewish and many of the names on my family trees do not appear to be either, but I am surprised and to be honest quite shocked how many Jewish names I've found on my family tree. It's a job researching them, learning the history of surnames and how they came about, when they came about, spelling changes, etc. Of course following the history of Jewish names led me to the Inquisition and I realized I had to write a book and document all that I had uncovered. I hope those denied of their truthful ancestry will cherish this book.

Please, do not be convinced that your ancestors were not Jewish just because they show up on baptismal records, or if they married in a church. I know it sounds strange and it's even hard for me too but you must look past that. They were living a secret life, to not participate in the local Christian faith would, (and often did) result in expulsion or worse. Even after the Jews were fully allowed to live in a country, they usually had to pay extremely high taxes that Christians were not required to. This was the case as well when Jews came to the New World colonies. A perfect example of continued persecution of the Jews was when New Amsterdam's (which later became New York) Governor Stuyvesant sent a letter to the directors of the Dutch West India Company, requesting authority to "expel" the Jews. Governor Stuyvesant tried to drive the Jews from the colony but his attempts were unsuccessful.

It's amusing to analyze family idiosyncrasies, the minute details of up-bringing, family ways of doing things and especially looking at prevailing family attitudes for clues. Does religious cynicism or skepticism run through your family? What was your family's attitude towards Christians or Santa Claus? Could you open presents before Christmas day? Did you have Christmas dinner on Christmas Eve or Christmas day and why? Did you open presents before Christmas? Was the art of preparing Mediterranean foods handed down to your grandmother and no one ever told you why? Separately these attributes prove nothing but together they form pieces of a puzzle. If your family has Jewish roots, you'll be pulled along.

The genealogical message boards are heating up regarding Jewish ancestry. It's lots of fun to read and watch people share information and piece together a picture of a Jewish family profile, especially when they speak of grandparents who had "Ladino" or "Yiddish" in their vocabulary. (Ladino is a mixture of Spanish and Hebrew, spoken by the descendants of Jews who fled Spain during the Inquisition and Yiddish is a mixture of "High German", Hebrew and Slavic.)

What psychological profile does your family have that ran through the generations? If we think in terms of the Inquisition, we can frame it. Think about it. How would you feel and how would your children feel and would not those feelings perpetuate through the generations? What kind of an attitude was there regarding authority, especially religious authority? Did your mother or father hold the clergy in high esteem or were they cynical and doubtful? Did they make way too big a deal of their Christianity, especially Catholicism? Did they seem to *fear* the church?

I've spent years piecing this all together and it's a lot of work but don't underestimate your piece of the puzzle. Even if all you have is one name, go a head and start an Internet family tree, someone someday may be very grateful that you did, as that one name could be the missing link, a bridge so to speak, to all the rest of the tree.

When you have some free time, go to ancestry.com. Go to "collaborate" then scroll to "message boards". You will probably be required to sign up but there will be no charge unless you desire their more advanced records. You can also type a surname in the search box and put "Jewish" in front of it, e.g.: "Jewish Brown" or "Jewish Jones". You are then able to read all the postings over the years where anyone has ever mentioned "Jewish" regarding the Brown family. I have read thousands of postings on ancestry.com that mention "Jewish". You get a great cross-section of all the different surnames that have Jewish ties. You will see many people looking for their great-grandparent's who "Anglicized" their name. It's astounding to read about all the North American surnames that have been altered.

Some people when coming to the New World gave themselves new names that had no connection to their ethnicity but enjoyed the sound of the name or adopted the surname of a prominent family or famous person. In those instances, you would appear to be following a false trail, but it may be the only information you have to go on. Scanning the genealogical message boards is a great way to explore this problem because descendants may have heard oral history about what a name "originally was" and what it was "changed to".

Here are just a few of the examples I've read while researching:

One immigrant in the 1880s took the last three letters of his last name and changed them to "ing" because the former "sounded Jewish and he could not get a job".

Polish immigrants were encouraged to Christianize their surnames to escape persecution and in another instance, the ancestor was "ousted by Jewish relatives" because he married into a Christian family.

Jewish families "practiced" Catholicism after they immigrated to the USA.

Families with "rumors of Jewish ancestry", but the family has been Catholic since the 1800s.

Children of Jewish parents who "married into Catholic families."

On the ancestry message boards, you'll read of oral histories that speak of families fleeing "over the Pyrenees Mountains", in the 1300s, to make their way into Holland "because they were Jewish" and the persecution in Spain was so "severe". Again and again you'll read of Jewish families going to the Netherlands, so much so that when someone tells me their ancestry is "Dutch", well of course it really lights me up. I have the surname "Holmes" in my family tree; it's a very English name. I saw a posting on one of the message boards where the first Holmes in their tree was "Jewish".

My father said our name "probably" used to have "berg" on the end of it. But he NEVER said we were German. He told me his ancestors came from Holland but looking back he never said we were Dutch either. Now I understand why. My family, like thousands of others went *"through"* Dutch lands but they were *not Dutch,* originally. Of course if a family was Jewish it doesn't mean they also weren't English, Dutch, German, etc. Napoleon said, the "Jews are a nation within a nation".

If you've read this far into the book, you know I would love to help untangle everyone's family chains. But first, you must *dispel any notion that they are not or never could have been of Jewish ancestry*. Just because one's ancestors are from "England" does not mean that their ancestors weren't Jewish. England, like most countries is multi-cultural. If you feel that "English" is enough then I suggest you quit reading now. This book isn't for you. This book is designed for those crazy genealogists and treasure hunters that want to go back just as far as they can.

Many of us have a variety of ethnicities in our family tree and researching them makes an interesting, colorful, valid way to spend time. Millions of us are able to piece together ancestry through the Internet and wide range of books available. Only those who have no idea of an ancestor's birth name or place will have difficulty but even these folks could have an enjoyable adventure with geographical locations and what history accompanies them. Carry on and do not let anyone stop you. Search, search, search for clues to your ancestors. Every little word or tidbit that we have on them is valuable. These are all pieces to the puzzle.

Digging through Internet articles, family trees and lore, I found my family tree well preserved. Names and images glare out at me from far away places. Like thousands of other Jews who fled the Inquisition, they often went through France, Italy or Germany before going to Amsterdam so they wouldn't attract attention by coming straight from Spain or Portugal.

Many of the Jews that were forced to leave Spain had previously (for their safety and security) converted to Christianity. Many knew quite a bit about how to pose as a Christian and probably even more knew how to keep their mouths shut. Perhaps it was during such trying times that the old saying, "don't ever argue religion or politics", became popular. For a Jew residing in a medieval Christian kingdom ... good advise.

Historians and genealogists will tell you that parents gave their children Biblical names because that was the fashion during the 1700 and 1800s. I always accepted that but today I am not so sure. I think we should reopen our family albums and look deeper into the meanings in our family trees and coats of arms. Names like Rachael, Levi, Sarah, Jacob, Benjamin, Hester and Ezekiah may have been the last opportunity American Hebrew parents had to lay claim to a heritage that stems back thousands of years and has Biblical bedtime stories to accompany it. Yes, my family is Christian as yours may be. But before that, they may have been Jewish.

"The Spanish and Portuguese names were to their gentile neighbors, a dead giveaway. The men may have dressed like the Dutch, trimmed their hair and beards like the Dutch and assumed Dutch aliases for business purposes outside of Holland, to protect them from harassment ... Their houses were done up in the Dutch style, and they prided themselves on their ability to pass as typical burghers in their new homeland. But there was no mistaking the distinctly foreign cultural flavor they brought to Breestraat."

Steven Nadler, "Rembrandt's Jews", University of Chicago Press

Chapter Two
The Diaspora and Inquisitions

Diaspora is the Greek word for "a scattering." An old dictionary I have, defines Diaspora in two ways. One definition is, "Jews scattered through the Old World after the Exile" and the other is "Jewish Christians of the apostolic age living among the heathen".

History puts a date on the first Diaspora from the Land of Israel (also known as the *Babylonian* exile) as 586 B.C.E. The Second Diaspora from the Land of Israel came after Christianity took hold. Jews that were not banished from the land of Israel packed up and left on their own accord. This scattering of tribes, clans and tents found their way into Southern Europe, Germany, France and Asia Minor. Archeological digs in Southern Europe have uncovered ancient Jewish artifacts dating back to the early Christian *Roman era* when Jews arrived as prisoners. Probably some of these prisoners regained their freedom and were eventually able to participate in Europe's cultural growth of art, religion, math and science. You may have never thought your ancestors lit candles on a menorah but they may have.

This dispersal to many parts of the world and the frequency with which Jews scattered repeatedly through the ages, brought about such terms as "Wandering Jews" or as what one genealogist quipped, "Wandering Presbyterians".

Jews went to Southern Europe in large numbers and helped build *The Golden Age of Spain.* During this era that lasted several hundred years before the Inquisition, various cultures lived in Spain peacefully (including Arabs and Jews) and respectfully shared their knowledge in astronomy, map-making, poetry, math, medicine, art, storytelling, religion, etc. The Jews partook of their communities, participated in their government, held powerful positions and together with Spain's unique blend of cultures shared their great wealth of knowledge. When the Spanish monarchy began envisioning their dream of a *United Catholic Kingdom,* and started *forcing* conversion, even by means of death, thousands of Spanish Jews dispersed again.

Most adults have heard the story of the *Inquisition.* Ferdinand and Isabella stated they expelled the Jews from Spain, because the Jews encouraged the "New Christians" to continue practicing Judaism. It was an ugly period of world history. The word inquisition implies the act of inquiring but it was much more than just an inquiry. Thousands of Jews were brought before a "judicial or official inquiry before a jury," and if found guilty of "judaizing" which could be anything from honoring the Sabbath on Saturday instead of Sunday or participating in anything "Hebraic", they were punished for *heresy*. An official "Holy Office" (tribunal) was established for the purpose of trials of such "heretics". There was enough burning, torture and forced baptisms to lead some Jews to suicide, (taking their sons along with them) and at the very least to hide, as best they could, the fact that they were Jewish.

For the crime of "Judaizing", the Monarch seized Jewish property, which left them with nothing. Subsequently, many Jews were taken into slavery or burnt at the stake. You can read a letter (www.sephardim.com) from the Catholic Church addressing the "pain inflicted on the Jewish people by many of our new members over the last millennium". It is a new era and today for millions, the Catholic religion is a source of strength and heart.

In 1391 and again in 1483 the expulsion of Jews from Spanish lands began and by 1492, Queen Isabella's desire to unite Catholic Spain resulted in *The Edict of Expulsion*. Ferdinand and Isabella gave the Jews three months to leave. All Jews were to be gone from Spanish lands by August 1, 1492.

The number of Jews living in Spanish territories at this time, is debatable, the estimates range between 100,000 to 800,000 people. Many of these families were situated in comfortable agricultural settings of pleasant orchards and fields of grazing cattle, enjoying life and culture with family and friends. This quick expulsion forced them to sell their possessions cheaply. The Inquisition forbade them to take any silver or gold out of the country, which left these Jews destitute.

Where did they go? One report has 120,000 exiled Jews going to Portugal because of a pact made with the King of Portugal but after six months they were expelled from there too and if they did not leave, they were made slaves of the king. Seven hundred (or more) children were sent to the Isle of Saint Thomas off the coast of Africa. Many other Jews fled to North African lands across the Mediterranean from Spain, (Morocco), and we must remember that France borders Spain so some families went there, escaping through the Pyrenees and settling in Bordeaux. Some went to Genoa, Naples and the Ottoman Empire (Turkey). Still others found their way into Switzerland, The Netherlands, Argentina, Brazil, Mexico, the Americas and some Jews wound up in Germanic territories in the early 1500s.

Details are available about this unfortunate situation. However, this book is not about the Inquisition. This book is about trying to trace our ancestry during a time when records were scarce. The dates of Spain's, Portugal's and Mexico's

Inquisitions are important. For example, if our ancestors suddenly show up in Italy, Turkey, The Netherlands, Mexico, etc., it becomes evident they were either searching for a better life or "displaced". The countries our ancestor's chose is important, as some were safe havens for Jewish refugees. Knowing the basics of the Inquisition, the dates, the lands, especially the names of the cities and villages where the Jews fled will help you in your search for your ancestry.

There was a lot of jealousy going on between the lower classes in Spain and the often well-educated New Christians (former Jews). Because of their education, they were given jobs within the Spanish government. The Spanish government was particularly fond of giving the job of *tax collection* to the Jews. Everybody loves the taxman... right?

The Spanish crown sought out Judaizers for many years. While much of the European world was colonizing the New World, including Spain, the Crown continued reaching into the New World colonies like Brazil and drawing out any "New Christians" guilty of "judaizing". It didn't take much to be convicted of judaizing and if a competitive merchant knew you were Jewish it wouldn't be hard for him to drive you away by informing the authorities in Spain that he noticed your wife didn't attend mass, or that he never saw you eat pork (against Jewish dietary law), or that he had noticed your child was circumcised.

In Spain, Italy, France and Mexico there were *border regions* that the historical records show were areas where Jews gathered and began rebuilding their lives. Jews fleeing persecution took the route through the Pyrenees Mountains to Bordeaux, France. The Pyrenees mountain range was a great refuge because the terrain was difficult for the authorities to travel through and enforce laws. Off and on, France forbade judaizing yet no Inquisition existed. Might one at least "regroup" there?

In addition, bear in mind such important dates as 1394 when France expelled Jews, and 1550 when there was a change of heart. If your ancestors show a movement pattern coinciding with these dates, it could be an important clue. Unfortunately, there's a long list of Jewish expulsion dates, from here, there and everywhere, readily available if you search for it on the Internet.

Many Jews converted and stayed in Spain or Portugal. Sometimes it was by force or fear of death. Other reasons made it impossible to leave their homes. Attached to Jewish converts were several names, "New Christians", "Conversos" or "Marranos". (Marrano meaning pig, because Jewish religious law forbade them to eat swine but they began eating it to show that they *truly had become Christians*.)

After the Inquisition drove the Jews from Spain, thousands of Jews went to Portugal where a new Inquisition soon took hold and once again, they were expelled. Next, they headed north toward the Netherlands. Some stopped and settled in Antwerp, Belgium where there had been a Jewish community since the 1200's. By the 1500's when the bubonic plague reared up, ignorant minds thought the Jews brought the plague because they weren't Christians, so once again they faced execution or expulsion. Today there is a very strong Jewish community in Antwerp, supported largely by the diamond industry. Diamond cutting is an intricate skill that many Hassidic Jews have mastered.

Many Jews took the trek farther north into the Netherlands. Let's take a look at Leeuwarden, Friesland, just about as far north as you can go in Holland without falling into the sea. Archeological digs have found homes dating back almost two thousand years and settlements used continually since the 1100's. Their coat of arms is a blue shield with a golden lion and a crown. There are varying thoughts on the origin of the name, Leeuwarden. Warden in Friesland's native language means "artificial dwelling hill" but the "Leeu" when put with "warden" comes out as

"Lion Dwelling Hill". If you already suspect that your ancestor may have been Jewish and they are from a hamlet called Lion Dwelling Hill that sports a coat of arms with a lion, you will be encouraged to continue along. If there's one thing the Jews brought with them from their old desert homeland, it's that remembrance of when *the lion roamed free about the hills of Judea.*

When searching for ancestral clues, buried for hundreds of years, we struggle to find concrete evidence. There are twists and turns along the road to filling in the blanks of our family tree and points at which we must make a decision on what to believe. So I will go on record as saying that it appears to me that Leeuwarden, Friesland hosted a Jewish enclave for a very long time.

Many Jews see Holland as a sort of *second Jerusalem*. It wasn't perfect for the Jews but the political winds blew enough in their favor to enable them to build new lives, particularly after the Inquisition when many Portuguese Jews who had been forced to convert left Portugal and went to Holland. In Holland, they kept quiet about their Jewish origins but eventually by the 1600s, they had become a part of Dutch society and built a beautiful synagogue that's touted proudly in today's Amsterdam travel brochures.

In 1571, a Mexican Inquisition began that lasted for over two hundred years. Any citizen who didn't have a certificate acknowledging the "purity" of their blood, *pureza de la sangre*, was in danger of arrest. There are quite a few books out lately about the "Crypto-Jewish" phenomenon. In the American Southwest, people are coming forward and expressing a desire to explore the customs of their ancestors who secretly practiced Jewish traditions and ancient religious rituals. Conversations on the ancestry message boards speak of the practice of Crypto-Jewish families sending their son or daughter to be priest or nun in order to appear Christian.

Families would name their children religious names such as Jesus, Mary Magdalene, etc. to keep the authorities off their backs, much the same way the Crypto-Jews of Spain and Portugal put swine in their food when it was against their kosher laws.

Keeping in mind that "New Christians" were often tightly-knit groups of "friends" and family, makes it understandable that once you get to your family tree you should see other Jewish names. Watch for the Anglicizing of a name. Look for even the slightest change of spelling and especially any surname change. In the 1700 and 1800s, cousins sometimes married. This could be a clue; *Jewish families wanted their children to marry other Jews*. No doubt, there are situations where the young couple may have been unaware that they were Jewish, yet both sets of parents knew.

Sometimes Huguenot's ancestors are in question as to whether or not they were Jewish, hiding behind the veil of Protestant Christianity. You could find yourself in a heated debate over this, especially if you have family members who pride themselves in their extensive knowledge of their Huguenot history. Study the names, deeply. There are plenty of resources where you can analyze a name. Find the meaning and what it was originally. Today, millions of Americans are signing documents with altered versions of Hebrew names, quite possibly both the first and last name. Huguenot and Sephardim Jewish communities backed up against each other and concentrations of Huguenots were in the north, south and west of France, near Spain where they would have recently fled the Inquisition. If you have Huguenot ancestry, I suggest you study their various websites and interesting history.

For those looking for ancestors during the 1600s, it's baffling to think of looking for Jewish ancestry in what later became Nazi Germany. It just doesn't sit right, but remember that Germany was a place you could get to by taking a boat up the Rhine River from Amsterdam. Think about how beautiful nature is and remember that to some of our early ancestors, there was no Germany,

France, Netherlands, etc., at least not in their hearts. They must have felt that they had every right to occupy a forest, a meadow or that gorgeous beach. We must sometimes remove the boundary lines so we do not confuse our current attitudes regarding nations and their politics with why our ancestors went where they did. Besides, a country's boundary changed rather frequently as new discoveries of resources prompted wars.

In 1885 Ernest George Ravenstein wrote these *Laws of Migration*:

Patterns
1) Majority of migrants go only a short distance
2) Migration proceeds step by step
3) Each migration current produces a counter current
4) Migrants going long distances generally prefer to go to a large center of commerce or industry
5) Major direction is from agricultural to industrial or commercial centers

Characteristics of Migrants
1) Females are more migratory within their county of birth; males more frequently venture beyond county boundaries
2) Most are adults; families rarely migrate out of birth county

3) Natives of towns migrate less than those of rural areas
4) Major causes of migration are economic

Volume
1) Large towns grow more by migration than birth rate
2) Migration increases as industry and commerce develop, and transportation improves

Though you believe your ancestors were Jewish, unless they were "protected" because they were "Court Jews", survival in Germany during the 1600s would have been difficult. Court Jews attained powerful positions of influence in European aristocracy. Whether they were bankers or money managers, consultants or representatives for trade or politics, they rose socially and received its rewards. Though not always permanent, Court Jews lived under noble protection and frequently received titles. Wealthy Jews used intricate networks to keep their sponsors well supplied with commodities and provided loans to Europe's middle class.

Mannheim Germany in the very early 1600s proclaimed "toleration" toward Jews in order to enlarge the city's population but Germany's openness for Jews became very dicey. It appears that protected Court Jews (the "HofJuden" families) built homes and lived openly as Jews but Jewish families accustomed to hiding were still reluctantly baptizing their babies and having Christian marriages. Jewish families, posing as Christians, would have been attracted to Mannheim's "more tolerant" attitude. The punishment for those *caught* practicing Judaism would not be as severe in Mannheim, which went back and forth with their policies toward Jews. There was a synagogue in Mannheim during the 1800s, which tells us that there was a love of that city along the Rhine and that Jews were eventually welcomed there before the Nazi era.

The barring of Jews from guilds (established by shopkeepers to protect against competition) made it impossible for Jews to have storefronts. This exclusion prolonged the history of the traveling Jewish trader who peddled goods door to door from a knapsack or wagon. "Protected" Jews though, made enough of an income to set up homes and continue their livelihoods as clerks for the municipalities. You will see the same pattern when Jews came to America. If the stories of your ancestor are that he sold goods out of a wagon, it could be that the family had survived through the decades and perhaps centuries, dependent upon that livelihood.

Since so many Jewish families had settled and built lives of excellence in Spain and Portugal, it is imperative that we keep the year 1492 embedded in our minds as a sort of median point. There was trouble long before the Inquisition but this is the era when we find hundreds of thousands of displaced Jews. Many of these ancestors that we envision during the 1700s pushing a cart around selling old clothes, may have originally come from a proud established European family. Survival was tough and many a sharp vendor immigrated to the Atlantic shores of North America where a new life awaited him.

Not all the Jews were poor, nor lived in great opulence like some of the famous banking families. There were those in between who wanted to partake of what society had to offer them so they continued living within a pre-established Christian framework. One look at a Jew selling rags on the street would be enough for a parent to return to his comfortable home and hide anything that might connect him to the ancient tribe of Judah, except, perhaps that glorious lion. When you go to Europe, you see lions frequently but not as much as when you enter Holland and draw nearer to Amsterdam. They are everywhere. And it is through the graciousness of many Hollanders, Jew and non-Jew that *the lion has prevailed.*

Chapter Three
Names, Laws, Rituals, Kinnui...

When people ask about the topic of this book, I usually tell them it's about names. A name is a little tiny song, and we hear that song almost every day of our lives and it was for this reason that most names have cadence as well as deep significance.

Ashkenazi Jews name their children after relatives that have died. Sephardic Jews also take great care in the choice of a name. Hebrew names get too complicated for the average person researching genealogy. If your ancestors have these great Hebrew names you may already know they were Jewish. This chapter is devoted to *deciphering* names in order to uncover Hebrew *roots*.

According to Rabbinical law enacted in the 1100s, Jewish babies (at the time of circumcision) must have a Hebrew name, "Shem HaKodesh" and a "kinnui". Jewish naming customs are complicated but it will help to remember that two names were used. The "Schem Hakodesch" holy name was used in Hebrew documents; it was taken at birth and used for rituals in the Synagogue. The "kinouy" (or kinnui/kinui) was a name that related to that person's immediate environment (a secular name). The kinnui name could be the same as the holy name but spelled and or pronounced in the vernacular, or the way the locals spoke. Sometimes the kinnui was an abbreviation of the sacred name. The kinnui is not a Hebrew name, though it may be a bastardization of it. For example, Kalman could be the kinnui of Abraham. A sacred name was much more popular for males than for females as women participated less in the synagogue.

Another example of Jewish naming patterns is the use of a "calque". Calque means "translation". The calque meaning is similar to the sacred name but taken from the local language. The calques were acceptable in legal documents.

Because for me this journey began with my ancestor *Jacob Lion*, and because Jacob is the patriarch of the tribe of Judah, I would like to begin this chapter with the name "Jacob". An ancestor with a name like *Jacob* stirs images of tents billowing in breezes sweeping across Middle Eastern desert sands. He is first *Yaakov* (Jacob) and then *Yisrael*. He is the son of Yitzhak (Issac) who is the son of Avraham (Abraham). And just in case you did not know, Avraham is at the top of both Arab and Jewish family trees, for he is their *Patriarch*. And it may help to note that the Polish spell Isaac as "Icik".

Judah means Lion. In the ancient past, a Jewish man could sign documents as either Judah or Lion. Lion eventually became a surname and we see it everywhere in its various forms, Lyon, Loewe, Garion, Leon, Leeuw, Luis, Luiz, de Leon, Luuesz, Lieuwes, Lieuwesz and on the "Sikh-Jewish Coalition" website, a message states that *Singh means Lion* in Punjabi (India).

The Jewish practice of changing the spelling of a name was very common. The name "Acaz" could be "Isaac" and "Epke" could be "Akev". Phonetically similar names can be frustrating because we are not familiar with the pronunciation of Hebrew names.

In the very early years of ancient Jewish society, there were three levels of society, "tribe", "clan" and "tent". The tribe was ruled by the patriarchal ancestor (judge/king) and meticulous lists of each generation were kept. The "clan" was ruled by an elder. The third level, the "tent" was a family unit.

Ancient Jews were referred to by their father or grandfather's given names. In the Torah/Bible, "Jacob" is referred to as "Israel". The names of his sons are used throughout history by both Christians and Jews. Here the list of Jacob's twelve sons: Reuben, Simeon, Levi, Judah, Zebulun, Issachar, Dan, Gad, Asher, Naphtali, Joseph and Benjamin.

Our Jewish ancestors covered their tracks because they were continually persecuted wherever they went and asked to be "quiet" about their religion. Yes, they were quiet with their voices but *they proclaimed it loud and clear through their Old Testament first names* and coupled with their surname (if you can trace back to the authentic version) we see who they were. We hear their pride. We see the evidence of early Americans building churches and building this country. What we can't see are their secret ancestors. Haven't you ever wondered why your ancestors just seemed to come out of nowhere?

A frequent message on genealogical message boards is that parents and other relatives "wouldn't talk about their Jewish ethnicity". They Anglicized their names, claiming their original surnames sounded "too Jewish". Jews who Anglicized their "Shereshevsky" name to "Sherry". Or they changed their name from the Russian "Cherne" (Black) to the German word for Black, "Schwartz". And I've seen an anti-Semite website that claims, "anything with a "z' is Jewish". Or the story of the Jewish man with the last name of "Cohen" who told his son he was hated by Americans during WWII so he changed his last name to "Craig".

I've seen Jewish genealogists mention that a name with the prefix Aven, etc. should definitely be seen as from the old Hebrew Abn, which is "son of". Aben, Aven, Avin mean "son of" and "Avinbruch" correspond to "Ibn Baruch", which is Hebrew.

The variety of surname prefixes and endings that came about in the Netherlands after the Inquisition could be a study in itself. There's "van" and "van de" or "van der". There's the French prefixes of "de", "d'" and "ver". There are the endings of "sz" or "x". The "sz" sounds Eastern European and could very well be, as during this period there were immigrants flocking to the Netherlands to take advantage of all the busy seaports and the work available. Those having the skills necessary to construct homes and businesses for Holland's wealthy merchant class would have found work. If they were Jewish they would have needed to hide it so they could join the trade guild. They would have hid it behind either Catholicism or Protestantism, depending on which one was *safer* at the time.

This scenario would have played out in any of the European countries and would follow the Jews to the New World. Whether arriving in Mexico or New Amsterdam (NY) they would surely have their paperwork in order, records of baptism, marriage certificate from a "church", record of christening, that sort of thing. One can only imagine how easy it must have been to counterfeit those crude documents but upon discovery of *improper paperwork,* many a poor soul was executed. I would never assume that an ancestor was *not* Jewish just because Christian documents exist. As painful as it was, they did what was necessary to survive. Remember, during the Inquisition, *thousands* died by being burned alive in the town square for all to see. Their crime, *Judaizing*.

Jews who posed as "New Christians" went to church just like all other good Christians. They studied the religion and went to confession, secretly keeping up their Judaism and passing it along through oral storytelling. It got harder as the years went on because the knowledge had to be kept hidden. The duplicity must have been very stressful, never knowing if your neighbors suspected, especially when they saw you "suspiciously" associating with other "New Christians", maintaining the ancient Jewish brotherhood of taking care of one another.

I know that not all lion icons signify a Jewish presence. However, they do symbolize the tribe of Judah and I'm sure that *some* do designate Jewish families or businesses and it is very exciting to see them. A trip I took to Israel included visiting ancient sites like Jerusalem, Cessarea, Armageddon, and tuned me into the fact that the *lion used to roam freely across the hills of Judah.*

That lion did not roam free in France where you see it often in old statues. When you travel north, just as many Jews did when escaping the Inquisition in Spain and Portugal, the farther north I got, the more lions I saw. By the time I got to Amsterdam, I saw them everywhere. The Dutch climate is a little chilly for the lion but thanks to the enlightened people of Holland, the lion roams free today.

I've seen it mentioned on an ancestry message board that, "Linhart means Lion Heart" and that "it is Jewish". If I had the time to investigate every new "clue" that came my way, I would study the ancestry of "Richard the Lion Hearted". He was the Englishman who fought the Saracens at Acre during the Crusades. According to the website, www.fleurdelis.com/coatofarms.htm, *"King Richard I changed his coat of arms from two lions combatant (or a lion rampant) to three gold leopards (or lions passant guardant)"*. Perhaps he just appreciated lions. He spent time in the Holy Land where there *were* lions. It's all very interesting.

In the past, varieties of spellings for a name were normal. It was not against any "laws". One genealogist goes as far as to say "spelling" didn't exist back then. Another professional genealogist says that her pet peeve is that beginning ancestry researchers are stubborn about sticking with the modern spelling of the surname. If you can't accept that the surname went through several metamorphoses, you'll not gain very much. And once you take a peek at sephardim.com you'll see many possibilities regarding surnames. Say you have the surname "Denyce" (De Nyse) and you go to sephardim.com to see if the name is listed as a Sephardic Jewish name. You'll see "Dente" and "Denis". If you say them carefully, you'll see they sound very similar. Or if you're researching the surname "Meet", you'll find "Mee" listed. Here is a list of historical surnames and next to it, the Sephardic Jewish names I found listed at sephardim.com. Please remember that just because a surname is listed on sephardim.com doesn't mean that all people with that surname are Sephardic Jews.

Bergens – Berga, Bergel, Bergamo
Carnine – Carnide
Coverts – Coviha, Covo
Demarees – de Marinas
Demotts – de Mota
Legranges – Legrain
Lists – Liz
Monfort – Monforte

Of course, there are many prominent Jewish families throughout history but two world famous surnames are Oppenheimer and Rothschild. During

44

the Middle Ages, when Jews were denied access to trade guilds they became dominant in finance and business, especially for the courts. This caused envy amongst other Jews whose lives were in sharp contrast and a fierce debate goes on to this day but the history of the "Hofjew" could play a role in your ancestry search, particularly if you see any clues in your genealogical tree.

One Dutch surname is "Brengerhof". In German, Hof means "farm or yard". Court Jews were called "Hofjuden", and whether there was intent to insult by association with a farm, similar to the derogatory "Marrano/Swine" name during the Inquisition, I have not heard but in the Netherlands "hof" meant "court" and the main messenger of this court was called a "Brenger". If your surname is "Brengerhof" or "Brinkerhoff" I would consider following the Jewish research trail. In England the expression was "Court Jew", and in Latin "Feret" means to "bear, bring, carry off, consider, get, produce, receive, tell, speak of or win". This class of Jews were granted "protection" because they were accountants, clerks, tax collectors, etc. who provided excellent service to the local government.

The common Jewish name, Moore, Mooris and its variants, has me wondering about the history of that name. The *Arabic Moors* were also driven from Spain during the Inquisition. The Latin word for Moor is "Maurus" from the Greek "Mauros" and in French you may find it as "More".

We are all familiar with the naming process whereby a son was named after his father, including Jews who accepted their father's name. Sometimes the name became long when the grandfather's name was also included, as in, *Jacob son of Tobiah son of Jacob*, that's one name!

If your Jewish ancestors correctly followed Jewish naming patterns, you could look at your family names and spot whether they were Sephardic or Ashkenazi Jews. Sephardic Jews were likelier to name their children after living relatives. The pattern goes as follows: first son named after the paternal grandfather, second son named after the maternal grandfather, first daughter named after the paternal grandmother, second daughter named after the maternal grandmother. Children born later were named after the paternal uncle or aunt and then the maternal uncle or aunt and sometimes after living siblings.

Ashkenazi Jews named their children after deceased relatives. If the mother died during childbirth a female baby received the mother's name, otherwise children were named after close relatives that had passed away.

Another common practice of ancestors who changed their name to assimilate into their new country, was to remove some of the letters of a name, sometimes purposely and sometimes through transcription. For example, one of my own ancestors who went by "Epke" was the son of Jacob Lion. I have found an Ancient Greek male name, "EPIKTETOS" which means *newly acquired*. If you look carefully, you will see that four of the letters removed, form the name "Epke". I have no idea if this is what my ancestor intended but it is an excellent example of what many Jews did to their names. Since we are on the subject of ancient Greece, let it be known that there were two schools of thought on the subject. Many ancient Jews loved the Greek culture and emulated it as best they could. An old Webster's dictionary defines *Hellenist* as "one who affiliates with Greeks, or imitates Greek manners; esp., a Jew who used the Greek language as his mother tongue." But the Jewish historical record also shows many Jews were opposed to the love of all things Greek as they felt it took away from Jewish culture. If you have some odd names in your family and don't know where they came from, look them up on the Internet in a Greek to English dictionary. Even my name, *Suellen*, as southern as it sounds, has its root in the Greek *Hellen*.

The generation lists from the Bible/Torah sit waiting for us. If not for the Diaspora, the generation lists might still be going, perhaps they are. I suppose the seriousness of that ancient generational list, is why during the Diaspora Jews tried tediously to maintain some kind of sign, though secretly, through their name, in the hope that they and their descendants would still be connected to *the tribe*.

To get a little feel for the names of the Israelite clans, who were the descendants of Jacob, we need only go to the Torah/Bible and read, "Numbers", the "Fourth Book of Moses". Here is where they named their tribes after legendary people. In Numbers 26, you'll see that Reuben, the eldest son of Jacob (Israel) is asked by Moses and Eleazar to "take the sum of the people". There are hundreds of thousands of people. But they begin an inventory and soon Hanoch's children become *Hanochites,* Pallu's children become *Palluites*, Hezron's children become *Hezronites*, Carmi's children become *Carmites* ... it goes on and on.

Napoleon is the fellow who insisted on surnames for his domain. Europe's population was growing despite all the deaths from disease, war and famine and he probably wanted to keep track of citizens. If a Jew was wealthy, he could purchase a name, a nice name like "Diamond" or "Rosen" but if he wasn't, he had a name given to him. One of my ancestor's surnames is "Kammerer" or "Camerer" and I'm not sure where the name originated but when looking into it I saw a reference to "Cameroon" which means, "crooked nose". Now that sounds like an assigned name and the meaning of which, if true, was never mentioned in my family.

I have Huguenot ancestors that I suspect were Jewish. It's interesting that common Jewish women's names, "Judith" and "Ester" were also common names for Huguenot women in Charleston South Carolina.

In his book "Rembrandt's Jews", Steven Nadler speaks of the popularity of the Jewess *Esther* and how during the Middle Ages, Amsterdam's Portuguese Jews saw in Esther, their own Marrano experience of being "forced to hide their Jewishness". The Jewish holiday, *Purim* celebrates Esther's story. The medieval Dutch loved to go to and produce plays about Esther. The Jews had their Esther/Purim plays, but kept Esther's name out of the title. The Dutch included *Hester* in the title and "went out of their way to make sure that no one missed the contemporary relevance of the drama", Nadler says. Purim is a Jewish holiday that celebrates the story of Esther. It begins at sundown on March 9th.

There are websites that will define names for you but I would not take their word as the final say. I think sometimes they just "took a stab at it".

And often it depends on *whom you ask*. Let's use the first name "Alvin" as a perfect example. Behindthename.com says it is an "Old English" name meaning "elf friend" from "aelf" and "wine" friend. But in an old dictionary, there's a section of "Common English Christian Names" and above Alvin is "Alvah" and "Alvan" and they list it as *Hebrew*.

The Jews of the Middle Ages were not unlike the Jews of Colonial America. They wanted to *blend in*. They frequently chose names from geographical locations or occupations and often had the same common names that were popular with the Christians of that area hence the difficulty in finding them now and the refusal for many to accept that their ancestors were indeed Jewish.

The way a name is pronounced is also telling, especially within Latino families. I spent some time recently with young children around the jungle gym at a local park. I was surprised at the abundance of Latino children with Hebrew names. Not only that, but when the parents spoke to their children, I noticed they used the Hebrew pronunciation. I spoke with one of the mothers who she said she was not Jewish. But as we got deeper into conversation, it became apparent that her ancestors probably were. By the time she left with her family, I could see that she was excited about revisiting her family tree.

There's definitely a movement underway to help genealogists meander through the tedium of the Inquisition. You'll find spehardim.com's resources impressive, thoughtful and brave as they are up against a wave of doubters, as are all genealogists. I have written a novel titled, *The Lies of the Lion*. The story takes place in Amsterdam during the Middle Ages. I bring these beautiful *post Inquisitional* people to light. I hope you'll read it.

Let's look at the surname "Nash". It's actually *Yiddish* and means "ours". The very Anglo sound of it coupled with its Yiddish history made it a popular name that Jews took after immigrating to America. The surname "Barkin" sounds English but it could have originally been "bar Cohen", which is a Jewish name.

Tobiau Israel da Silva is a good example of a true Sephardic Jewish Portuguese name. If you see a name like this on your family tree, you will have a lot of fun following up on it. Derived from Latin, "Silva" means forest. There's a claim posted at ancestry.com stating that "Silver is not English but derives from the Portuguese De Silve, Da Silva, Silva, etc". Silva is one of the most common surnames in Brazil thought in large part due to the practice of giving common surnames to freed slaves and native-born people.

Except for the fact that my father-in-law is Jewish and I had been researching and discussing Jewish genealogy with him for many years, the website, www.sephardim.com is pretty much where I got started. This website lists both the original Jewish name and the "alias" that was used. I find it a great place to familiarize with Jewish research.

Through the ages, people became very creative in the ways they altered their names. Many non-Jewish names managed to become popular Jewish names but Rabbis were strict about which names a child could use. They were concerned over the practice of naming Jewish babies gentile names and set up creative ways for Jews to have both a sacred Jewish name and a name that fit within the local culture. This sacred name was what descendants could use to recognize that their ancestors were Jewish. It's unfortunate that too often, these sacred names became lost or abandoned.

My focus is on Jews who separated from the main body of Judaism. These "New Christian" families did not outwardly attend synagogues and if they gave their children "legal" Jewish names, they probably did not speak them out of fear of persecution. It may sound strict that Rabbis would impose "legal" names for babies but even today in

Portugal and other countries, there are laws regarding what names are appropriate for newborns.

If you were forced to convert to Christianity *and* forced to come up with a new name, what would you do? How could you rebel without being killed or exiled? Some Jews had no desire to take Christian names so they drew their names from nature by picking plants, bushes, trees or chose the names of places. Many surnames that are *colors* were chosen by Jews rather than picking Christian ones.

The use of multiple names is a Hebrew tradition. Jews blended common German names with Hebrew names. Hebrew names were important for legal contracts but the ancestors that we are looking for were probably long past writing up Hebrew contracts. They were hiding their Hebrew origins and at what point they quit teaching their children Hebrew probably varied within each family. In the 1800s, it became popular in Germany, Hungary and Poland to give Jewish children local common names. It was quite common all over the world, to take the name of a town, city, village, hamlet, etc. Just because the ancestor you're researching doesn't have a Hebrew, Yiddish or Ladino name does not mean she wasn't Jewish.

Because choosing surnames from geographical locations was so popular, there are a tremendous amount of surnames surrounding Picardy, France. Picard is a region in northern France, complete with its own French dialect where Jews and Huguenots developed communities after fleeing the Inquisition. You've probably seen the surname Picard, Picard, Pickart, etc. If you have that surname you could ponder whether your ancestors resided in that area and whether or not were Jewish.

If one of the surnames you're researching is the name of a village, definitely research the history of the village. Did the village exist at the time your ancestor lived? Naming a child after a geographical location was popular and is still practiced today.

We are looking for clues wherever we can find them. Dig deep. Investigate each and every locality your ancestors were known to have lived. Get the dates and find out the politics of the times. You might find that they left at about the time a law was enacted against Jews or occupational regulations prohibiting them to conduct business, etc., or that they arrived shortly after a decree was enacted *welcoming* them.

Find family trees on the Internet that have the same last name. Comb through looking for ANY

Jewish names. Jewish families stuck together. If you are having no luck, take one name and research it deeper, going farther and farther back looking for any period where there was a spelling change or a name change. Conversos often took the name of their "Godfather" so go back as far as you can and be open minded. DO NOT CLOSE ANY DOORS. Look for names on ship's passenger lists. Look for any similar names in the rosters of Jewish merchants. (See "Notarial Records from Amsterdam's Portuguese Jewish Community that Mention Danzig" www.jewishgen.org/Danzig/amsterdam.php).

Here is an example of a last name I garnered from someone else's family tree that is phonetically similar to "Wroten", one of the Dutch surnames I'm researching. The surname "Ruttan" derives from a Jewish family tree. These "Ruttans" migrated from the Netherlands to the New York area, which fits with my being told that my "Roten" ancestry was from the Netherlands but *not explicitly Dutch*. This Jewish surname, "Ruttan" sounds very much like the Sephardic Jewish name listed on ww.sephardim.com "Rotin" and also the many variations of the name, Roten, Rotenberg, Roughton, Wroten, Wroughton, Roaten, etc. This "Ruttan" was born in 1564 in Saint-Mihiel, France. What a great clue. What were the politics in Saint-Mihiel France in 1564? Was it a border village? During the Middle Ages, Jews tended to live in border villages and along seaports so they could flee easily.

My "Roten" ancestors had a rice farm in Eunice, Louisiana, Cajun country. Before they moved to Eunice, they bore a daughter in Mississippi that they named Eunice. For years, I have wondered if there was a connection. Recently while I was reading the ancestry message boards, I saw a story about a Sephardic Jew with the surname of "Nunez". This family line began in Jerusalem, bearing what name, I do not know but they fled to Spain then to Portugal then to Savannah Georgia. Eventually this Nunez surname became "Eunice" because it sounded so similar to the Spanish Nunez/Nunes. Savannah Georgia is not very far from Eunice Mississippi. For more on the surname "Nunes", go to ancestry.com where you'll find a posting from a man who was born in Portugal. His fascinating story surrounds the oral history of his "Nunes" family whom he says was originally "Ben-Nun". He states that his Nunes family line went all the way back to the days of Nebuchaneezer (the king of Babylon who conquered Jerusalem).

It may seem outlandish to think that someone could piece together a family tree spanning back more than 500 years before the advent of Christianity. But given the fact that many oral histories have proven accurate, we should consider all possibilities and respect the *ancient word of mouth* as unique and promising.

There's another posting I read where a family can trace their family tree back to 1150. Their coat of arms is "a lion standing on back legs holding the Star of David in its claws." On another genealogical message board, someone has posted information regarding the surname "Baca". This person states that "Baca is Hebrew" and means, "to wail". Their oral history also states they are from the royal house of King David.

It is not one circumstance but all the circumstances presented together that form the picture of your origins. The names are not like physical artifacts that may become chipped or broken; they are more ethereal and can be pieced together again.

Obviously there were Jews who were not forced to convert to Christianity but embraced the religion on their own. If they were trying to cleverly leave a remnant of their Judaic name, it had to be discreet. In other instances, the requirement to choose a new name wasn't taken seriously and they made up some ridiculous names. And who is to know whether someone chose the name of a bush or flower because they loved nature or because they did not want a *Christian* name?

You need to decide where you believe your Jewish ancestors *settled for a while* because the longer they stayed somewhere the more they took on that culture. The Jews that went to Spain and Portugal *loved their Iberian identity* and were devastated to be driven away. If they were only there for a year they wouldn't have absorbed much of the culture but if they had been there for a hundred years their names would have been Latinized, or Africanized as in the instance of the Afrikaner language. (Many Jews went from Holland to South Africa, their descendants are still there today, and like some Americans they may not know of their origins.)

Each country has its own patronymic or matronymic style of names and that information is readily available on the Internet. In the Portuguese language, "es" added to the end of the patronymic surname as in Nunes, designates "son of" as it does in Spanish when the name ends in "ez" or "iz". This was not the original way but the practice existed during the Middle Ages. Other examples of endings in other languages that mean "son of" are, "sen" and "son" as in Mendelson, or "sohn" as in Mendelsohn.

Patronymical surnames were used during the Middle Ages in the Netherlands. "Son of" was "se", "sen", "szen" or "z". An "x" or a "dr" at the end of a name meant "daughter of". "Van der",

"Van den" and "Van" designate the family hails from a geographical location, for example, "Van den Einde" signifies this family was *of the end*, and "de" simply means "the". "Te" would mean "at".

The suffix "ovna" in Russian designates "daughter of" and "ovitch" son of. "Ben" also means "son of" in Hebrew as does "Aben", "Aven", and "Avin". Take the prefix "Ibn" (Arabic) or "Abn" (Hebrew), they both mean "son of", so the Italian name "Avanzino", could be from a family of Jews that fled Spain or Portugal during the Inquisition and went to Italy (which thousands did) and the name morphed over the years. Avanzino would then mean "son of Zino". I ran across a reference to an Italian mapmaker, "Zino", during the Middle Ages. This of course would fit, as the Jews were known mapmakers and astronomers. I've read history books that surmised that Christopher Columbus's mapmaker was Jewish and it was to his credit that Columbus did so well at sea. There are also many who wonder if Columbus was Jewish, or a Converso.

And as a little side note on Italian Jews, I saw a clip from the book, "The Jews in Genoa: 507-1681" by Rossana Urbani and Guido Nathan Zazzu. The authors state "During the Middle Ages the Jews lived mostly in Chiavari or Sestri Levante working as barbers and surgeons." I find it interesting that the "Levante" is also the name of the region where Lebanon, Syria and Israel are located.

During the Inquisition, thousands of Jews went from Spain to Mexico. Unfortunately, the Inquisition eventually followed them which necessitated *they conceal their ethnicity*. When I look at Mexico, I see the beautiful blend of ancient North and South American indigenous cultures as well as a rich Arabic and Jewish influence. They shared their knowledge of science, math, music, religion, food preparation, spices, candle-making, glass blowing, weather predicting, cloth dying, weaving, creating new pigments for painting and learning new languages that gave the ability to share all this information.

The coastal area of Mexico is where many Jews settled during the Inquisitional period. As the years progressed, many moved toward the cities. Descendants portray ancestors as Jews who posed as Christians. They chose highly religious surnames like "de Jesus". They allowed their daughters to become nuns and their sons to become priests so that the family could go to him for confession, avoiding the Catholic version of confessing sins. These families were guilty of Judaizing and they could have been executed for it. History shows that thousands were. These ancestors kept their Jewish symbols hidden away, perhaps never showing them to their children. There is a long list of Converso surnames from Mexico and America's Southwest. The descendants of these Crypto-Jews are speaking up and re-claiming their heritage and it is not always easy for them.

There is no shortage of entertainment in the genealogical message boards. There's even a James family that believe they are Jewish and that their ancestor, the notorious outlaw Jesse James was "half-Jewish" *because Jesse James mother was a Lithuanian Jew from Ireland.* And sometimes I wonder if people aren't making this stuff up but I haven't found evidence of that, not on genealogical sites. The people who post are for the most part helpful in every way they can be. There's a sense of family among many, calling each other "cousin" and checking in from time to time to wish all well. If you're lonely and need a sense of belonging... go to the message board of your surname and start a thread. If there isn't one with your surname, start one up. If you were adopted or have no family, there are message boards where they discuss ancestry of various states, like the Mississippi message board or Texas and there are numerous websites dedicated to the same. There are so many websites, I suggest you find a few that you like and stay put. Believe me, some sites are a lot better than others for navigating around. You make friends too and share email addresses if you wish. The surnames their family members marry into provides more clues as well.

Those with the surname "Moore" (Mooris, etc) should enjoy embarking on their historical journey. Before Ferdinand and Isabella began with their "United Spain" idea, the Moors (Muslims) had been living comfortably within Spain right alongside the Christians and Jews. Spain was a wonderful place to be. A competition between scholars led to some of our current knowledge of math and science. Medieval Spain cultured music, dance and philosophy. Before the Inquisition, Arabs and Jews discussed religion openly and freely. Landowners included Jews who had ranches where they raised cattle and grew olives for oil. They lived well. When the Tribunals were instituted, the Moors were also forced to convert. And if Muslims became Christians and Jews became Christians, no doubt there was intermarrying. So, are we to wonder if some of our Jewish Morris surnames aren't also of North African origin?

Egyptians enslaved the Jews and the Mongolians conquered vast sections of Eastern Europe. Some historians believe that the Vikings traveled to ancient Phoenicia where they brought their sea-faring skills to the hills of Lebanon. Some of the Melungeons of the Appalachian Mountains have an oral history that they are Portuguese and some have ancestors who placed the Star of David on their tombstones. Some descendants of *Converso Portuguese Slave dealers* in Colonial America wonder quietly if their ancestors were Jewish.

What genealogist doesn't enjoy studying their family coat of arms and trying to decipher the hidden symbols they may reveal? A coat of arms is a nice addition to anyone's family history. I have even seen them as newly created, so it's never too late for your family to have one, although an ancient one probably exists out there, *somewhere*.

There are those, who like their ancestors, desire to leave Judaism behind. Unfortunately, this wish to leave it behind is often due to the hatefulness of others and as we know, it led to a history of abandonment of Jewish names. Even today, there are rude people who find their way into the ancestry message boards but the fact that many clues *are decipherable* gives me a sense that our ancestors trusted in a future when freedom as well as intelligence would prevail.

While researching the Inquisition, I discovered the derogatory use of the word *Hebrew*. As in, "The shopkeeper was found to be Hebraic and was called before the Inquisition." The word "Hebrew" was used frequently back in the Middle Ages. I like the word. I think it's a beautiful word. I once had someone ask me, "Can I say the word Jew? It's not a bad word is it?" You may laugh at that but there's such truth in that candid question. It's perfectly fine to use the word Jew; the Jews use it all the time.

In the 1640s, Brazilian Conversos from Portugal played a role in the marketing of slaves. As odd as it seems, one might be able to make a bridge to Jewish ancestry through the atrocious slaving industry, keeping in mind that to some Jews it is very offensive and *not* historically accurate to imply that Jews were the "main" slave merchants but American surnames going back to the Colonial era often have Portuguese origins.

I wonder about every name I encounter, including my own. My first name is Suellen. Another common spelling is Sue Ellen. It definitely sounds *Southern*. I used to leave it at that but not any more. Ellen is derived from the Greek "Hellen". "Su" is Spanish and means "his, her, its, your, their, one's" which could translate as "your Hellen" or any of the other variants.

If my father's family were Jews who became "New Christians", who became *New World Colonists with Anglicized names,* I'm going to analyze Southern traditions in a different light. For instance, how did the Southerners develop the custom of double names? Could it stem from Jewish naming patterns? Could the southern name, "Jim Bob" be from the ancient tradition of Hebrew naming patterns? *We have to brainstorm to get through that brick wall.*

We must not leave out the Scots and the Irish. The two countries are close together and each take pride in their different cultures but because of their close proximity, there is an overlapping. We even have the term "Scots-Irish", a lively group who came to the early American colonies with the hope of a better future. Their surnames are abundant on the *Dawes list of Native American names* because they frequently intermarried with the Indians. There are also Jewish surnames on that list.

The surname "O'Connor" sounds Celtic but it only means *descendant of Connor.* Could there be a connection to the Jewish surname Coen or Kohn? There are researchers on the Internet that insist that the Scots were from the tribe of Judah. It is my understanding that the coat of arms of the old kingdom of Scotland was a lion. "McManus" is another Celtic name and it literally means *son of Manis.* You will find the Jewish surname "Manis" on the records of *Bevis Marks, The Spanish and Portuguese Congregation of London.* (sephardim.com)

One day I saw a website that claimed that Celts were descendants of a mix of several of the *Twelve Tribes of Israel*. A peek into the dictionary revealed the following:

Hibernia – Ireland
Hebrides – Group of islands off the west coast of and belonging to Scotland
Heb., Hebr. – Hebrew(s)
Hebraic – pert. to the Hebrews or their language

Proponents of this theory insist that the Irish descend from the *ancient Hebrew tribe of Dan* and that the Irish tribal name of "Tuatha de Danaan" identifies them. They go further and state that the Danite symbol is the eagle and that they discovered America twice, once in the B.C. era and then later as Vikings. Today the eagle is America's iconic symbol.

At a large Celtic Festival in my community, I've noticed Jewish booths set up to share their heritage amongst the kilts, sword fighting and beautiful damsels. There's a tribal movement underway and the technological age offers the whole world an opportunity to compare oral histories and family documents... in real time. Share those letters you have in that dusty box. Talk to your grandfather while he's still around. Go to the library with a few notes in hand and look things up. Get on the Internet and go where you're led. The ancestry message boards are full of folks who say things like, "No one would ever speak of our being Jewish," or "They won't tell me a thing". Perhaps *you* can help them connect.

"Until mandated by laws enacted in the late 18th and 19th centuries (the date varies by country), most Jews did not use fixed surnames. Jews with a common given name were often distinguished by a patronym, meaning that a father's name was used in addition to a given name. For example, Jacob the son of Abram was called Jacob Abram or Jacob ben [son of] Abram. If this was not enough to distinctly identify a person, a nickname was used. Such nicknames described a person in some way, such as a physical characteristic, occupation, or place of origin. A Jew named Abram ben Maimon might also be called Abram the copper merchant or Abram red-beard. These nicknames were not permanent or inherited. They changed from one generation to the next. Fixed surnames often developed from these patronyms and nicknames."

https://wiki.familysearch.org/en/Jewish_Names_Personal

Chapter Four
Following Historical Trails

I grew up with a sense of not knowing my origins. Now why was that? You would think that if there were nothing to hide I would know. And if you haven't noticed, there are many Americans that don't really know where their ancestors hailed from, which is why genealogy is so popular in this country. Who are we?

Take my maiden name for example, Wroten. It's an unusual name but was never spoken of being Jewish. Once I saw "Rotin" listed as an ancient Sephardic name, of course I began researching in a different direction, one not mired in the illusions of fairy tale knights and English Royalty, as so many Americans are obsessed with. And I don't see "English" ancestry the same way either. So what if our ancestors were in England before they came to America, and so what if they were a knight or held some other noble title, they could still have come from Jewish ancestry. Plenty disguised their identity before going to England. But let me show you how it could work.

Many descendants of the big family of Wroten (Wroughtons, Raughtons, Rowdens, Rowdans, Rodens, Rotin, Roden, Roten, etc.) believe they stem from one fellow, Ezekiah Roden born in the very late 1500s in Dorset, Dorsetshire England.

We know what boat he came on when he arrived in 1631 to Jamestown. So we have four things we can research, the first name, the last name, the boat he came on and where he came from.

For starters, "Ezekiah" is a very biblical-sounding first name and we have been informed that "Rotin" has ancient Sephardic origins. "Hold it", you say, "Lots of Christians have biblical first names, that was popular back then". But let's take a look at the name Ezekiah. (H)ezekiah was the son of Neariah, who descended from the royal family of Judah and you can find this in the Bible in the Old Testament book of Chronicles, III: 23. So the origins of both his first and last name have ancient Hebrew origins.

Let's research if any Jews were living in Dorsetshire England in the late 1500s, when Ezekiah Roden was born.
(Using an Internet search engine with the following: *1592 Dorsetshire England Jewish*)

A quick viewing of an article, "The presence of Africans in Elizabethan England", reiterates points I already know: the Portuguese "New Christians" or "Conversos" were accustomed to having slaves. They continued with their commercial networks from Amsterdam, Antwerp and Constantinople. There is reference to the Portuguese New Christians (*former Jews*) who "took refuge in

England in the 1540s." So yes, our "English" ancestors could have been "New Christians" or *Crypto Jews.*

In the late 1400s and early 1500s, Jewish settlements were banned in England. By 1656, Jews "openly" settled in England but they were still not officially allowed so they may have hidden behind the facade of Christianity. It appears that only prominent Jewish families in England before 1650 will be found in the historical records.

Let's look at the fourth factor, the boat from London that Ezekiah came over on, the Bona Nova. Let's run "Jewish Bona Nova" through a search engine and see what comes up. Not much. So there are no references to Jews being on the ship the Bona Nova coming from England in 1619. Right now, all I have to go by is the very Hebrew nature of his name, Ezekiah Roden and that Jews were in England in the late 1500s. By the way, a look in the phone book in Israel will bring up many Rotens, Rotenberg, etc. and there is a very famous cookbook author, Claudia Roden, who wrote the "Book of Jewish Food". It appears she is Jewish as are others with that name. There's also a Benjamin Roden, who was involved with the "Branch Davidians" in Waco, Texas. Ben is a Hebrew prefix meaning "son of". Benjamin, means "the son of my right hand".

Back to Ezekiah. One of his wife's surnames was Berman. Not exclusively a Jewish name, there are other European origins of Berman but I do want to note that Berman is also a Yiddish (Jewish) name that means "Bear Man".

Who was this Ezekiah Roden? If the Wrotens were originally Jewish, they have blended very well into the Colonial environment of the New World. If the name originated from the old Sephardic name Rotin, they Anglicized it to Wroughton etc. and have hidden it well. Many African Americans also bear the Wroten name and are searching for their ancestral roots. Wroten/Roten family lines have left records of having household and agricultural slaves, perhaps just a few but enough to have left a legacy within the African American community. The pattern, in which they kept housekeeping slaves, resembles that of ancient European Sephardic Jews.

Many family histories dead-end with Huguenot history. When I run across discussions on genealogical messages boards, "They were Huguenots" is often the last word we hear of our ancestors, or sometimes it is the way their story begins. If one can have the wisdom to look beyond the claim that their ancestors were "Huguenots", you may be able to dig much deeper into your family history because not all Huguenots were Huguenots. Many Huguenots were actually Jews, mingling within the Huguenot communities because they felt safer being a Protestant than a Jew and, many were not interested in becoming Catholics. An in-depth investigation into possible Huguenot Jewish connections would be quite interesting. Even though many years have past, there are still plenty of clues to be found.

Huguenot is what the French called the group of Protestants who preferred to call themselves "Reformes". Forty-three years after the Spanish Inquisition of 1492, the Catholic Church ordered the extermination of the Huguenots. The Reformes were tortured and killed. Eventually the Reformes (Huguenots) became the Calvinists, as they followed the French Protestant Church founder, John Calvin. In Holland, the Calvinists eventually became the Dutch Reformed Church.

The Scribner-Bantam English dictionary describes Flanders as "the medieval country in Western Europe along the North Sea, now divided between Belgium and France". Flemish refers to Flanders and the language is Low German of northern Belgium. Thousands of Huguenots (who fled France after 1598) went to this area, as had Jewish refugees in 1290 after England's King Edward I, expelled them. The Huguenots had secret meetings in Flanders. The secret bible studies were called *Huis Genooten*, which means, "house fellows" or *Eid Genossen*, which in

German means "oath comrades", as they were bound to each other by an oath. This reminds me of the ancient Jews and their brotherhood and of secret societies like the *Knights Templar* and today's *Masons*.

There are those who believe that Jews posed as Huguenots. One family researcher mentions that their ancestor was born Jewish in what is now Belgium but was "publicly" a Huguenot. Yet as a "Huguenot" he was persecuted so he went to Holland, then to England then to the New World Colony of New Amsterdam (NY). Jewish families may also have posed as Huguenots in the late 1600s when the Huguenots are recorded as immigrating to South Carolina. Barbados's sugar plantations provided great wealth for many of the new immigrants to South Carolina. It was this wealth that created the image of the wealthy southern gentleman farmer and his plantation.

I believe there were Jewish families (perhaps "New Christians") who came to the colonies from New World places like Barbados, Jamaica and Bermuda. They immigrated to South Carolina and became farmers, including rice farmers. Later, many rice farmers left South Carolina and settled in Louisiana. Whether these Jewish families were public about their origins or not, by the time they wound up in Louisiana, the only remnants of their Semitic background may have been those old

Biblical names. And when the slaves sang their beautiful *Spirituals*, how many were aware that they had Jewish ancestry?

Before the Civil War, history records the southern Jews as keeping silent about the morality of slavery. But during the revolution of the 1960s, thousands of young Jews fought for civil rights and helped African American citizens obtain the equal rights they deserved. The fight for equality is not over. Today, many Jews continue to devote their lives to the politics of freedom.

Who were the Acadians? Were they Jews too? One woman on a Jewish message board came from a Catholic background and she had recently learned that Acadians may have originally been Jewish. She was uncomfortable that she had not known the truth. The Acadians were a former French colony in Canada, now known as Nova Scotia that "ceded to Great Britain 1713". Webster's Dictionary says, "ceded" but I think more accurately the Acadians were thrown out. Most of them went to Louisiana and are known today as *Cajuns*. The area where the Wroten's had their rice farm, Eunice Louisiana, is Cajun country.

And where did these "Acadian" people get their name? One has to wonder if they are not the "Ak'kad" people.

"Akka'dian" – Of or pertaining to the ancient Semitic inhabitants of southern Mesopotamia before 2000 B.C.E. or to their civilization, or to the east Semitic dialects of Babylon and Assyria."

"Mesopotamia" – region in ancient country, Asia, between Euphrates & Tigris rivers; in modern, usage practically coextensive with Iraq. Where some believe the biblical *Garden of Eden* existed.

Approximately seven thousand recorded Jews fought with the North in the Civil War and approximately 3,000 recorded Jews fought for the South but there must have been many more American Civil War soldiers of Jewish ancestry than history records. As I mentioned before, the history books record Jews in America as not speaking out against slavery. They were very quiet about it. As was the case in Bergen County, New Jersey when right before the Civil War the county had a pro-slavery attitude. They expressed it when they did not vote for Abraham Lincoln as President. And in South Carolina where large populations of Jews had settled before the Civil War, the Jewish community did not speak out against slavery, possibly due to ties to Conversos from Brazil etc. who may have directly or indirectly provided for their livelihoods through the slaving industry. In other words, if you have several clues that lead you to suspect your ancestors were Jewish and they hail from South Carolina, you may be on the right track.

In the summer of 1654, twenty-three Jews came to New Amsterdam (now New York). They stand historically as being the first Jews in what later became America. They had come from Recife, Brazil. These twenty-three Jews left because the Portuguese conquered Recife. Less than two-hundred-years earlier the Inquisition had ruined the lives of hundreds of thousands of Jews. Once again, they were terrified about their Brazilian future when the Portuguese conquered Recife so these twenty-three Jews headed for Holland. Through an odd course of events, Spanish pirates captured the ship, which was then recaptured by a French privateer ship. The twenty-three Jews from Brazil were taken to New Amsterdam (now NY).

These twenty-three were ill received by governor Peter Stuyvesant. He did not want the colony to "be infected by people of the Jewish nation". The Dutch West India Company literally *owned* New Amsterdam (now NY) and the company had a nice share of Jewish stockholders. The company told the governor to allow the twenty-three Jews to carry on their business but they were to exercise their religion in "all quietness". I am sure that there were a lot more than twenty-three Jews in New Amsterdam back in 1654 and there were plenty more to come. When

NY was the Dutch Colony of New Amsterdam the Jews probably went by Dutch names or Hebrew names altered to the local area. When the English took over and the colony became New York, the new Jewish arrivals, once again arrived quietly and went by Anglicized versions of their Hebrew names or changed them all together. No wonder we are unaware of our Jewish ancestors with all the quietness expected of them.

During the Inquisition, the southern area of Holland, the Belgium area and Amsterdam, become heavily populated with Sephardic Jews who had gone north and Ashkenazi Jews who had come from the east. Many of them kept their Jewish identity private. Sephardic and Ashkenazi merchants helped to bring about Amsterdam and Antwerp's prosperous Golden Age, through elaborate trade connections that still existed with Portuguese traders.

In 1604, the first town in Holland that officially opened up to Jews and gave them freedom to practice their religion was Alkmaar, a community approximately twenty-five miles from Amsterdam. The next year, Haarlem offered Jews land where they could bury their dead and stated that Jews could dress as they wish without the need to wear any symbols that distinguished them as Jews. And if Haarlem, Holland was welcoming to Jews, it seems fitting they would settle in New Amsterdam's, "Haarlem".

It is a commonly held belief that the majority of American Jews are the descendants of those who came through Ellis Island in the late 1800s but did the accidental arrival of the twenty-three "first" Jews to New Amsterdam (NY) draw out some of the "Dutch" who were really "Jews"? Did these "quiet" Jews in New Amsterdam began to mingle with the newcomers who were up front about their ethnicity while others continued to blend in with majority ethnic groups? This could be the reason why both Christians and Jews share the common New York surnames of Ackerman and Voorhees.

Discrimination against Jews continued in a variety of ways, making many Jewish citizens uneasy about revealing their origins. It was not just Shakespeare and Stuyvesant who stirred the pots of anti-Semitism. Jews faced these negative stereotypes wherever they went, so please be patient and understanding when trying to uncover who your ancestors really were.

You might wonder how your ancestors came by the resources necessary to make their trip to the New World. They may have financed their journey through their occupations as Hofjude or "Court Jews". Court Jews purchased cut diamonds for the nobility, from Jewish merchants in Amsterdam,

Antwerp or London. By the early 1700s, many Jews went to London because the diamond trade formerly in Amsterdam went full swing in London. The Jews opened "cutting houses" and became expert "diamond polishers". These surnames could be derived from the occupation of Hofjude or "Court Jew": Coerts, Bringer, Brenger, Brengerhoff, Feret, etc.

Here's a perfect example of how someone might go about researching to see if their ancestors were Jewish:
I have an acquaintance whose grandmother's family is Portuguese. Because thousands of Jews fled Portugal during the Inquisition, "Portuguese" also often meant "Jewish". So of course, I wondered, could this young woman's ancestors be Jewish? The surname she gave me was "Pacheco".

The first thing I did was go to www.sephardim.com to their 'Sephardic Names Search Engine". They list: Pachao, Pacheco da Costa, Pacheco de, Pacheco Leon de, Pacheco Tavares, Pacheco, Percheco, with the references to back it up. It looks promising doesn't it? However, just because the name Pacheco is listed at Sephardim.com does not mean her ancestors were Jewish. If we don't find any more clues, we will get discouraged and give up. Nevertheless, if we keep finding more and more clues we come up with a profile of this family. It's up to the individual whether or not to speculate or assume that they were Jewish.

I looked for Pacheco on the Paris Census for the year 1292 and did not find it. When I looked on the list of names of Jews paid to leave Amsterdam, there was Pacheco. I found the clues quickly and was moved forward and very excited about this family name. I also googled "Jewish Pacheco" and came up with many websites pertaining to Jews with the name of Pacheco, including one person searching for their maternal Pacheco Jewish link. But this still does not in any way prove that Pacheco is only a Jewish name and we may never be able to prove that. However, if we can get the first name and any other names associated with this particular Pacheco family, we will begin putting the pieces of the puzzle together.

As I mentioned earlier, I have my suspicions that Friesland in the Netherlands during the Middle Ages was a "Crypto-Jewish" enclave. Jews fled to Amsterdam to *lay low*, why would they not have done the same in Friesland, especially since it was even more remote? Friesland's language is also different than throughout the rest of Holland and the Dutch are reported to have a hard time understanding them, and deciphering what their Christian names mean. Could this be due to the confluence of cultures that settled there?

You are able to access thousands of family trees online. Studying several Jewish family trees will give you a sense of their patterns. Make up a timeline and get the feel for where they went, then when you look at your ancestry line and where they went you might find a pattern. For example, look at the following passage from www.chn-sife.nl/pages/chn.htm:

"Leeuwarden obtained town-rights in the year 1435 and became capital city of the region in 1504, when the central government and jurisdiction settled down here. Beside that, Leeuwarden became the residence of the Frisian stadtholders. In these centuries the town was flourishing. The number of inhabitants rose spectacularly: from five thousand in the year 1500 to sixteen thousand in 1650."

The Netherlands was one of the most important destinations for the Jews leaving Spain and Portugal during the Inquisition and the above paragraph provides several valuable clues. Many of them went from Spain to Portugal and then when Portugal began expelling them they went to the Netherlands. Now we have MORE questions. The Netherlands was a place where many Jews changed their religious identity. They loved the Netherlands because it wasn't Catholic. And many became absorbed into the Huguenots as they both had the same enemy, the Catholic Monarchy that sought to eradicate them. Next would be a research of the history of the Huguenots. Who were they? What did they believe? Where did they migrate? Are there any clues in their belief system that hint at Jewish origins? Once the Huguenots arrived in America or the Caribbean what happened? The Huguenots were not Catholic so many of them may have assimilated into other Protestant denominations. Arriving in the New World meant carving a life out of the wilderness and creating a "house of worship". Communities may have already had a church, and many people go with the flow.

Over the years Cryptic Jewish families lost the knowledge of their faith. Families lost not only the rituals, but also the knowledge that the family was once Jewish at all, especially when they were constantly being told by the authorities to be "quiet" about it. Life was hard for these families; they struggled with disease, war, famine, etc. The younger generations may have been left with only the basics; love God, be kind to your fellow man and honor the Ten Commandments.

On further research on Leeuwarden in Frisia, the Nederlands, I have found the following at http://tuupovaarankoulu.jns.fi/comenius/hollanti/k ulttuurisivu/cultlw.html:

"Weapon, Name and Flag. In 1818 under French administration was decided that the Weapon of Leeuwarden should have the following shape and colours: blue, with a climbing Lion of gold; the shield covered with a golden Crown. The color blue probably represents the sky or heaven. Gold represents of course the sun. The name Leeuwarden has something to do with the Saint Vitus Cultus. The Dutch word "Leeuw" in Leeuwarden means Lion. We believe that Saint Vitus was thrown to the Lions in the Middle ages by emperor Diocletianus. Saint Vitus made a cross-sign with his hands and instead of eating him, the lions started to lick his feet. After several attempts to kill Saint Vitus finally the emperor succeeded killing Saint Vitus by burning him in a oven. Afterwards Saint Vitus became a Saint and the people worshipped him as a Guardian angel of the cities and villages. The Leeuwarder Flag has 4 horizontal stripes from top to bottom: blue, yellow, blue and yellow."

What have we here? The French give Leeuwarden the color "blue, with a climbing Lion of gold, the shield covered with a golden Crown." Besides the Star of David, Israel's flag is composed of two large sky blue stripes on a white background. The blue stripes represent the blue stripes on Jewish prayer shawls that men wear during prayer. Of course I have no idea who the "French" authorities were who "gave" Leeuwarden this flag design. My imagination can come up with any number of ideas. But hey, I write novels too.

I just cannot help the nagging feeling that Friesland was a Jewish refuge during the Middle Ages. Read this excerpt from "Names, Names, & More Names: Locating Your Dutch Ancestors in Colonial America," by Arthur C.M. Kelly, that is available to read at ancestry.com:

"The provinces of the Netherlands are extremely small but each continues to keep its own distinct character. The Province of Friesland has a different language so that other Dutchman have a difficult time in understanding them. Family names in Friesland generally terminate in 'a' as in Van Cysingha, Kingma, Camminga, Van Heemstra, and Postma. Their Christian names are also peculiar and don't lend themselves to easy translation. Men named Sjoust, Jouwert, and Skato and women named Wietkske, Vrouwke, and Tcota are not unusual."

Did Jews fleeing the Inquisition in Portugal bring Portuguese nicknaming styles to the Netherlands? An Internet search for hypocorism brought up Wikipedia where they discuss the usual hypocoristic Dutch endings:

http://en.wikipedia.org/wiki/Hypocorism

"When the name is ending with a t or a d the ending is then a -je (e.g. Bert - Bertje). Is the final consonant of the name a m the ending is then -pje (e.g. Bram - Brampje) -metje (Bram - Brammetje) or -mie (Bram - Brammie). For the other consonants the hypocoristic form is -tje. In the southern parts of the Netherlands the hypocoristic form is often in their dialect a -ke (e.g. Peer - Peerke). Also in the Frisian the usual hypocoristic ending is a -ke (e.g. Ype - Ypke). But this forming (and others like -ske and -tsje) often makes the name feminine (e.g. Jetse - Jetske) like in Dutch (e.g. Jan - Jantje, Hans - Hansje). There is another productive hypocoristic ending: in the eastern part of the Netherlands (mostly in the province Drenthe) the female form is -chien Examples is Anne - Annechien, Lammert - Lammechien.
a parallel construction in Portuguese, with -(z)inho/-(z)inha, as in Aninha from Ana and Joãozinho from João."

It is at this point that one begins to feel that *the more they know, the more they don't know.*

Keep searching, searching, and searching. Use the Internet. Search Wikipedia.com for the country and the village. Dig deep. Go to Google.com and put "Jewish" in front of the last name. Search for a coat of arms, put "Jewish" in front of place names too.

If you find an example of a Jewish family tree from the same country your family came from, study the first names. You will become familiar and develop a sense for Jewish names and the pattern. Remember, in the past, it was not uncommon for cousins to marry, that happens in family trees of all ethnicities but it could also be a clue if a family was Jewish and they wanted their children to only marry a Jew.

I can't believe how many times I have found something very interesting in a place where I was searching for something entirely different. The same goes for helping others with their family searches, their "old country" history could prove a clue to your own.

Once you have pages of notes, it's easy to cart them around to Grandpa's house so you can ask questions and write his answers in the margins.

Your notes might contain information that triggers his memory.

During the Inquisition when Jews fled Portugal and settled in Amsterdam, they were referred to as "Portuguese Merchants". Some of the non-Jews understood that these "Merchants" may be "Jewish" but as long as they kept "quiet" about their religion there were no problems but as soon as Jews gathered for their funeral processions or otherwise loitered in groups it was frowned upon and they were asked to stop. By the time Jews arrived in the New World, they may have been accustomed to being "quiet".

Many of the early colonists (who were converts to the Dutch Reformed Church, "Calvinists" and whose parents or grandparents had been Jews from the Inquisition) continued to conceal their Jewish origins. Since the New York area was such a birthplace for America, if the colonists who came from Holland were not Christians but Jews, who cultivated huge families and partook of the building of a nation, it's fair to say that America was built on a much stronger Jewish foundation than what was originally thought by historians.

Excluded from guarding the town, Jewish Immigrants to New Amsterdam (NY) in 1655 were required to pay a special tax instead. In 1655, Asser Levy, one of the first Jews in the colony could not pay the tax and wanted to stand guard. The authorities said no. Asser Levy persisted and finally received the right to stand guard. A couple years later Asser wanted to be a "burgher" (citizen) and the New Amsterdam court (NY) said "No" but through his persistence and that of other Jewish leaders, they eventually gained the right to be burghers. These are the names of four of the early leaders of the Jewish community in New Amsterdam (NY); Abraham De Lucena, Jacob Cohen Henricques, Joseph d'Acosta and Salvador Dandrada. You'll notice that they are Jewish names yet sound Portuguese or Spanish.

During the Middle Ages, when Jews were kept from joining trade guilds they often partook of these occupations: running flour mills, fur-trading, inn-keeping, peddling (with packs on their backs or carts/wagons), banking, accounting, clerking, diamond cutting and diamond polishing. They also became Rabbis. Jewish pawnbrokers and merchants were sometimes referred to as "bankers". In the late 1800s when Jewish immigrants began arriving in America by the hundreds of thousands, they brought these occupations with them.

I displayed an old portrait of a beloved ancestor, to someone in a genealogy group who replied that he looked "sub-Nordic". I assume he means *not Nordic,* meaning geographically below the Nordic area. I scratched my head at this, still confused until I read this paragraph in Abba Ebban's book, "HERITAGE, Civilization and the Jews":

"In one of them alone, Auschwitz, 3 million people, nearly all of them Jews, were done to death. In the summer of 1944 alone, 400,000 Hungarian Jews were murdered there. This monstrous outrage was accomplished by Nazi Germany against humanity in the name of an idea – the idea that to destroy the allegedly "inferior" non-Nordic peoples was a noble task. But the Holocaust was enacted in the midst of a Europe ostensibly rational, scientific, and civilized. It was accomplished mostly in the war, but it was independent of the war. It began before, and it would have continued after ... if victory had not gone to the Allies."

Abba Ebban speaks of Hitler and the term "non-Nordic". I realize the person who said my ancestor looked "sub-Nordic" was ruling him out as Nordic but could they be using the term "sub-Nordic" derogatorily? You may unwittingly find answers to some of your questions about Jewish ancestors from anti-Semitic people and places. You will need to ignore the hatefulness.

The Jewish name "Cohen" has traversed the globe. Some Afrikaners share the surname "Koen", originating from the Jewish "Cohen". Afrikaner-Jews are called "Boer-Jode". At the beginning of the 1800s, Ashkenazi Jews from Britain and Germany immigrated to South Africa but many people of Jewish ancestry had already settled in South Africa in the 1600s, having come from Holland. You will find Yiddish words buried in their vocabulary. You may find a similar situation among South Africa's Protestants, many whose ancestors were originally Jewish but today their descendants know little of it.

As the Jews wandered from country to country, they took with them their dietary customs but adapted them to the region in which they currently resided. (For a more in-depth look into traditional Jewish foods, read, *The Jewish Mama's Kitchen*, by Denise Phillips.) The Ashkenazi Jews from Poland, Russia and the Baltic, ate Borscht (beet soup), cabbage and barley soups, stews, stuffed vegetables and hearty, starchy, sugary, comfort foods because of Eastern Europe's long, cold winters. The Sephardic Jews from Spain and North Africa ate lighter, spicier foods like kebabs, rice and salads because of their warmer climate.

Jewish dietary laws were strict, forbidding shellfish and pork. The term Marrano arose from Jews adding pork to their traditional dish so they would not appear Jewish, so we know they broke Jewish dietary laws. Don't think that because your grandfather ate pork he wasn't Jewish.

In 1590, just over the border from Texas sat "New Spain". Today, it is the Mexican state of "Nuevo Leon". There's that lion again, Nuevo Leon, *"New Lion"*. Monterrey is the capital of Nuevo Leon. The founder of Monterrey was a descendant of "Crypto Jews". The Inquisition killed him and over one hundred of his relatives because many of the family members returned to Judaism. For more information on this google: *Crypto Jews Monterrey Nuevo Leon.*

There is a reason for the colloquial expression "Wandering Jew". Jews immigrated all over the world. They went to Turkey, Iraq, Poland, Germany, Holland, Austria, Russia, India, Afghanistan, Pakistan, Kashmir, Myanmar, China, Switzerland, Mexico, America, Brazil, Argentina,

France, Spain, Italy, England, Egypt, Iran, and Portugal ... the list goes on.

There are reports of the Lost Tribes of Israel traveling the *Silk Road* and settling in the areas of Pakistan and Afghanistan. Though the descendants of these nomadic people have now become Muslim, they continue to marry only amongst themselves, light candles on the Jewish Sabbath and have other customs and characteristics that are very Jewish. The Bani-Israel, which means *Children of Israel*, has an oral history that states they were taken from their desert homeland. They have a legend that Jesus did not die on the cross but traveled to the Kashmir valley searching for the Ten Tribes and it was there he died.

If you are interested in the claim that the Scots and Irish have ancient Jewish ancestry, there is an Irish legend that Noah's granddaughter, Cessair had been refused onto the ark (along with Finian) so she led the first people to Ireland. Only Finian survived.

Also of Jewish genealogical interest is Zeeland, in the southern part of Holland. During the Middle Ages, Middleburg, Zeeland, with it's clothing and wine industries and the affluence of the Dutch East India Company, was a happening place, not far from Amsterdam, which shined brightly during her Golden Age.

It's not just fun to find a famous figure in your family tree; it's valuable because famous people are likely to have a more complete family tree. I'm interested in "Manasseh Ben Israel", Amsterdam's famous Jewish scholar and orator, beloved by Jews and Gentiles. He was born with the Portuguese name "Manoel Dias Soeiro". I saw similarities between his genealogy and my ancestor's, "Marie Sohier". The names are phonetically similar and the families were in Holland during the same era, which couldn't have been that heavily populated back then. The surname, "Sohier" is not exactly "Soeiro" but my experience has shown me that spelling changes were more common than not during the Middle Ages. Today we will occasionally find these names Anglicized as "Sawyer".

Menachen Ben Israel was born about 1604 and his family went to the Netherlands. Marie Sohier was born about 1630 in Nieppe, Hainault, France. Ben Israel came from a *Marrano* family. History records Marie Sohier marrying into a Huguenot family who fled to Holland. Marie Sohier's family had close ties with a family known as the "Uzilles". Manasseh's education was under "Rabbi Issac Uzziel".

Even if such a fun hunch proved false, I see it as a perfect example of names that are phonetically similar but written differently. And to add to the mystery, Manasseh Ben Israel's father's name may have been "Gaspar Rodrigues Nunes". We can add that to the interesting surname file of Nunez/Nunes/Eunice.

"Conversos emerged as a dominant force in the areas of finance, commerce, international trade, law, diplomacy, and all levels of public administration. Wealthy Conversos purchased and endowed ecclesiastical benefices for their children with the result that many members of the high clergy were of Jewish descent."

Benjamin Netanyahu

"Once the ex-Converso community established rabbinic Judaism they began observing Jewish precepts and prohibitions, developed over many centuries, which regulated and restricted relations between Jews and Gentiles. Regardless of this, there is evidence that some ex-Conversos men took lower-class gentile women, often maidservants, as mistresses. From 1600-1623, notarial records reveal instances of sexual relations between Portuguese Jews and gentile women (most of them were Dutch or Scandinavian). Even though it was illegal to have sexual relations between Jews and gentiles under Jewish and Dutch law, few of the ex-Conversos or their mistresses were prosecuted."

Frank Longoria

Chapter Five
Conversos, Marranos and Slave Traders

After the Inquisition, Jews who resided in Christian countries, feared exposure for secretly practicing their religion. It's reported that these "Crypto-Jews" worshipped in their own fashion with the doors and windows tightly shut. There were no holy books to be found and no Rabbi to facilitate. They were *on their own*. They had Christian names and gave Christian names to their children. They attended mass. Out on the streets they were Christian but inside their home, they "Judaized". This separation from formal Jewish instruction necessitated creativity that sometimes led to the development of superstitious practices.

Remember the self-flagellating albino monk in Dan Brown's "The Da Vinci Code"? I saw a posting on an ancestry message board that stated that the Catholic Penitent Sect stemmed from Crypto Jews who were trying to display their Christianity. I suppose this is similar to making a show of their conversion by adding pork to their traditional Jewish stew. Once again, Jews leading double lives, in secret they practice Judaism and in public, Christianity.

By the Middle Ages, the world had witnessed thousands of years of slave trading, rape and pillage. Even under these circumstances, people fall in love. It was not prohibited for blacks and whites in Spain to join the Catholic Church or to intermarry. Their Mulatto descendants became respected artists and lawyers who fit into Andalusia Spain's intellectual circle.

The history of slave trading is ancient and no culture is innocent. Packing people in ships and selling them for profit is disgusting and sad. Though the enslaved lived through pain and suffering, many lived to bear children and those children bore children. For many of us, those early slaves were our ancestors. For many of us, the slave traders standing over them with a whip were our ancestors. For many, the slave and the slave owner *both* were our ancestors. Our job is to find out who our ancestors were and hopefully to love them. If you find that an ancestor was a cruel, heartless person who did terrible things, be glad that you have a huge family tree. Everyone has members in their tree that did both great and evil deeds, though we probably wish to keep quiet about those relations. We might want to rationalize the unscrupulous characters we have in our family tree but leave no doubt, our ancestors really mixed it up.

The first African Americans came to the colonies as Indentured Servants and in the early colony of Virginia were comfortable intermarrying with Native Americans. The Portuguese, who had made their way very early to the Appalachian Mountains, were also comfortable intermarrying with the other two groups. (Many researchers believe the Mungaleons of the Appalachian Mountains descend from ancient Jews who came from Portugal on a boat). Sometimes Spanish women took African men as lovers and husbands. In the Northern Mediterranean, black slaves were favored over white slaves because black slaves more readily became Christians and assimilated easily into Spanish culture.

In the late 1500s, Scandinavians began immigrating to Holland right along side German immigrants. There was plenty of work available in the seafaring ports and towns. The Scandinavians were tall and blonde. These were the "Old Norse" people, Norwegians, etc. But so were the "Normans" who conquered Normandy and in 1066 so famously captured England. Nevertheless, when we see people today who attribute their ancestry as from "William the Conqueror", they aren't usually tall and blonde. But blondes pop up occasionally in families of brunettes, etc. reminding us of the variations in our ancestry.

According to Thomas Cahill in his book, "The Gifts of the Jews", ancient Jews were short and had black curly hair. Today we have some very tall Jews, brought about through intermarrying and better nutrition through the ages. We have blonde Jews too. Understanding who we are and where we came from fosters a healthy mental state. It makes us strong and can bring great joy. If you don't like what you find out about an ancestor, research another one. Have fun with finding where you fit into this beautiful collage of humanity. You will never be excluded. You are a part of the human family.

Searching for ancestry can also bring sadness. My joy at finding that I belonged to this huge family tree that spread out from America to Europe and into the Middle East was dampened by someone else's family name I was researching, Chaya. While I had just finished scrolling through hundreds of names of my family, the lives they led, their politics and pioneering, their loves and their losses, their prosperous industries, I then scrolled through a Chaya website where there were many names in this family tree with the inscriptions, "killed in the holocaust".

The brother of one of my ancestors was "Seba". The name could be short for Sebastian or I could read more into it, and start getting into the Bible/Torah. It amazes me that the ancient Hebrews were recording family trees thousands of years ago. Seba leads us to Noah who begat Ham who begat Cush who begat Seba. Noah's son Ham figures interestingly into the issue of ancient slavery. During the Middle Ages, both Christians and Muslims believed that the descendants of Ham had turned black because Ham's father, Noah, cursed him because Ham was drunk and naked. During the Middle Ages, Catholics and Calvinists believed it was this curse of Ham that made it acceptable to enslave people with black skin.

Easton's Bible Dictionary   Seba: One of the sons of Cush (Genesis 10:7).
The name of a country and nation (Isaiah 43:3; 45:14) mentioned along with Egypt and Ethiopia, and therefore probably in north-eastern Africa. The ancient name of Meroe. The kings of Sheba and Seba are mentioned together in Psalms 72:10.

One of the more interesting books I use as a reference is, "Atlas of the Year 1000", by John Man. On pages 72 and 73, there is a map depicting ancient slave origins and trade routes. I was shocked to see the map had little red dots (I counted seven) marking the locations of "castration centres".

In 1613, the Dutch built a trading post on Manhattan Island. Around 1625, England set up operations in the Caribbean but still very few African slaves resided in the colonies along the Atlantic coast. Indentured Servants (usually Caucasian) were the norm. Indentured Servants, both men and women were bound by contract to a master or landowner for a specified number of years before they were granted their freedom. So, we indeed must throw them into the mix. Indentured Servants came from locations around the globe, including England, Spain, France, Scotland, Ireland and we should never forget the Slavs for this is where the word *slave* originated. Some of the ships that brought Indentured Servants to the New World had deplorable conditions and harsh treatment. However, by 1626, Caucasian Indentured Servants were no longer the norm. At this time, the West India Company began supplying slaves to the early colonists.

We have a period in history, along the Atlantic coast, where Europeans, though usually at war with, on occasion lived peacefully with their Native American neighbors. The European men (especially Trappers) sometimes took Native American women for their wives. A Native

American woman, who spoke in her native tongue and had the knowledge of hunting and terrain, was an asset to a Frontiersman, especially if she kept her connections with tribal members. As the years progressed, the Native Americans inter-married with Africans because they often found themselves living on the same plantation as slaves. And on occasion, the Jewish, Dutch, English, French and Spanish landowners took slave women as their wives or concubines. These slave owners were able to give their mulatto children a good education and a higher standard of living (though due to the hard working slaves). Many of them went on to marry white people or other light-colored mulattos, eventually the dark pigmentation disappearing leaving later generations to not know they had an African American 11th great-grandmother.

By the 1700s, the whole world had gone crazy with slave trading and it was mostly the selling of African slaves. You could invest in slaves like people bought tech stock in the 1990s. Fortunes were made and until the 1730s, the Portuguese were the kings of the Atlantic slave trade.

Because Spanish and Portuguese "New Christians" or "Conversos" became involved in slave trading and massive agricultural businesses that found their way onto American shores, someone with Southern ancestry might follow history back far enough to find Jewish ancestry. Remember, not all but many of these "Conversos" or "New Christians" were still proud and fond of their Judaism and when caught were executed for practicing it. They built big empires and amassed great wealth with their plantations along Africa's coastline and into the interior. They colonized the coast of Brazil and the West Indies and the Caribbean Sea. Barbados and Jamaica were used as stopover ports where cargos of humans were revitalized before going to the early colonies along the Atlantic and the Gulf of Mexico. Again, some of these "New Christians" and/or "Conversos" of Jewish ancestry intermarried with Native American captives, African American captives and Scottish, Irish, Italian, German Indentured Servants. Before the middle 1700s, there were well over thirty thousand African Americans in South Carolina. South Carolina began cultivating rice, the planters needed experienced agriculturalists, and the enslaved Africans provided that. In the north, Rhode Island depended on Jamaica and Barbados for molasses to make rum. There was an amazing growth of agricultural endeavors closer to the equator that eventually spread to the warmer southern areas that we now know of as Florida, South Carolina, Louisiana, etc., which brought the practice of multi-ethnic sexual relations, both consensual and non-consensual.

Hugh Thomas, in his book, "The Slave Trade" speaks of how during the 1750's and 1760's Newport Rhode Island was North American colonies most important slaving zone. Thomas writes that Newport "always welcomed enterprising people without asking whence they came," and that, "Newport used more slaves in small businesses, farms or homes than any other Northern colony did" and he also states that the most interesting Newport Rhode Island slave merchant (in 1762 he entered) was Jewish Portuguese, Aaron Lopez. "He had concealed his Judaism in his youth in Portugal and came to North America in 1752..." In the beginning, Lopez was a "general trader, operating from a shop on Thames Street, selling everything from Bibles to violins, being especially concerned in the trade in candles ..." He entered the slave trade in 1762 with his father Jacobo and brother-in-law Abraham Ribera. Lopez was known as a successful philanthropic and highly regarded.

During the 1600s, Spain used its Inquisitional power on Portuguese Slave Merchants as a political and economic tool. The Portuguese had grown enormously wealthy with their ventures into Africa and South America and Spain did all in its power to control the competition. Historical documents from the Holy Office at Cartagena de Indias show some of the Inquisition's investigations.

The history of slavery goes back for eons but to a great extent, the Portuguese began kidnapping North African Moors from fishing villages during the middle 1400s. The Portuguese found that the Senegal River flowed from the West African goldfields. After 1445, as the need for labor to mine the gold escalated, they began to purchase slaves. Rarely did the black, Muslim Merchants trade in Muslim slaves but sold into slavery, people they acquired from raiding other tribes. The influence of the Moors brought about the Spanish Vaquero that led to the American cowboy.

During the early years of human exploitation, there were civilized people living along Africa's waterways, not in the sense that we speak of civilized today with our hot showers and running water, but large empires where they had built up strong trading networks. They were weavers with the cotton they grew and dyed with indigo. They fished and made butter and traded in bananas using gold for money. There were markets where slaves were sold, right alongside horses. African slaves were purchased by Portuguese traders and resold after returning home.

In Spain, it was not unusual for the working classes to have slaves and definitely commonplace for those of upper classes. Laws were enacted to protect slaves from sexual misconduct but children were born of slave women and these children often became legal citizens with all the same rights as other Portuguese. In the case of Lancados, (Portuguese men who adopted the African culture and lived among the Africans) children they fathered with African women became an asset for them in their settlements.

There wasn't just gold and goods coming from Africa. European goods were going to Africa as well, obtained from the ports of Antwerp and Lisbon and by 1500 the industries of African slaves, sugar, grape wine and rum were well on their way. The Portuguese and the Spanish competed for wealth obtained through the exploitation of Africa's resources and its people as slaves. The story of Sao Tome and the sad fate of Jewish children, whose parents were taken as slaves because they couldn't pay fees after the Jews were expelled from Portugal, appears prominently in all the Inquisitional stories. The children were taken to the island southwest of Africa's Cameroon where they were used to build sugar plantations. What happened as the years progressed to these Jewish children and their descendants, I have never heard. Some of them no doubt inter-married with descendants in Africa, unaware of their history over five-hundred-years ago. Perhaps a few were taken as wives of the Portuguese industrialists who were developing the sugar industry and their descendants now live a life of wealth and privilege after generations of sugar profits. Some of the children may have eventually befriended and perhaps wed the Portuguese "criminals" that had been the first settlers to the island.

In Spanish America during the early 1600s, it was thought that mulattos were the result of breeding white Moor slaves with black slaves. It's also important to point out that historians say there were no bonds between the various African tribes. I have heard that repeatedly, especially in the context of white Americans who feel defensive about early American colonist's role in slavery. You will hear, "Well, the Africans sold other Africans". This is true. All the ethnic groups throughout history made use of people from other tribes to do all the miserable hard work. It's a sad fact.

There are accounts of the Portuguese New Christians in Africa and the Caribbean being persecuted for Judaizing. The Portuguese "New Christians" who were profiting heavily in the slave trade around the time of Christopher Columbus are a huge genealogical link that spans from many locations, not limited to but including Spain, Portugal, Holland, Italy, Malta, Africa, Brazil, and the Caribbean Islands to our early colonial North American shores. And we must consider the captured natives in North and South America and all the islands in the West Indies. While reading

"The slave trade: the story of the Atlantic slave trade, 1440-1870", by Hugh Thomas, I began collecting surnames of reputed Converso slave traders; Elvas, Enriquez, Morin, de Andrade, Barreto, Prieto, de Robles, Mesa, Acevedo, Sevilla, Peres, Febos, Lamego, Conchillos, de Noronha, de Loronha, Mascarenhas, Jimenez, Rodrigues, Simon, Caldeira, Caballero, Jorges, Lopes, Lopez, de Sevilla, Mendez de Lamego and perhaps Gomes Reinel, de Cordoba, de Ceja and de Jaen, Angel, and Duarte.

Jews were scattered all over the world. There were Jewish communities in Brittany long before the Anglo Saxon invasion and after the Romans invaded Jerusalem. I've read that the Romans returned to ancient France (Gaul) and took Jewish prisoners to Lyons, Arles and Bordeaux. Paris is reported to have had enough of a thriving community in the 500s to support a synagogue. But in the middle 1100s, anti-Semitism became a serious issue in France. Jews had to pay a tax on Palm Sunday and in one city, Toulouse, where they practiced burning at the stake, the church called Jews in weekly so they could "box their ears" to be reminded of their guilt.

King Philip, who ruled over a large territory, imprisoned all the Jews and asked for payment for their freedom. He voided loans in 1181 that Jews had made to Christians but not without first taking a profit of the voided loans. In 1182 King Philip confiscated Jewish possessions. He then drove the Jews from Paris, allowing them to return sixteen years later if they would pay fees and special taxes. Life must have been hard enough for the average person trying to survive in France during these early years, consider these difficulties when doubt creeps in as to whether or not your ancestors were Crypto-Jews. Then in 1215, the Jews had to wear a badge in the areas of Normandy, Provence and Languedoc.

It's understandable that Jews would flee the persecution in Spain and Portugal. But have no doubt; Jews in France received much of the same hatred. When aggressive Christians descended on French villages of Anjou and Poitou in 1236, several thousand Jews were killed only because they refused to be baptized. It was dangerous to be a Jew. What would you do? What did they do? They hid their ethnicity but not entirely and it's up to us to uncover it.

Remember these dates, they may fit in with your ancestor's comings and goings. In Northwest France (known as Brittany back in 1240) the political powers drove the Jews out. They were readmitted later but in 1305, Phillip IV rounded up all the Jews and confiscated all their possessions. One-hundred-thousand Jews were driven from

France, fortunately ten years later Louis X accepted them back in France.

During the middle 1300s, many Europeans blamed the Black Plague on the Jews. There were all kinds of crazy stories that people fabricated about the Jews and again in 1394 Jews were driven from France. It wasn't until the middle of the 1500s when Jews were accepted again in France. Many of the Jewish immigrants to France were "Marranos" from Portugal and reportedly, most of the "Marranos" eventually accepted Christian lifestyles.

Around 1648, Jews left Poland (and the Ukraine) and went to "free" French port cities in the south (near Eastern Europe). Your family tree might start showing Eastern European-sounding names around this era. They would contrast with Latin-sounding surnames (Portuguese, Spanish, Italian, French). This could signify Ashkenazim marrying Sephardim.

Bordeaux is a French city that comes up a lot when researching Jewish ancestry. Because of its proximity, north of Spain and Portugal, many Sephardic Jews fled through the Pyrenees and settled in Bordeaux. In the 1700s, both the Sephardic and Ashkenazi Jews took up residence in Paris. The Sephardim are said to have been "wealthier" probably due to an intricate network with successful merchants in Amsterdam and elsewhere, perhaps even through or indirectly because of the wealth made through the Atlantic slave trade. Even into the 1700s and 1800s, there were incidents of persecution against Jews in France that would lead Jews to seek a better life across the seas in America. The French Revolution gave Jews the right to citizenship in late 1790 and early 1791.

"There were times when it was safer to be a crypto-Jew overtly practicing Catholicism than to be a Huguenot, but in the earlier years (up to about 1572) it was safer to be a crypto-Jew overtly practicing Protestantism than to be an overt Jew... Others, of course, are hesitant to believe in or acknowledge Jewish ancestry because of their strong and prominent membership in the Christian culture ... In the United States, and more so in some specific areas such as Charleston, South Carolina, the Huguenots intermarried with prominent other Protestant families and became full members of the Christian (mostly Protestant) aristocracy. As in other areas of crypto-Judaic studies, research in this area is hindered because of reluctance of some descendants to acknowledge either overt or covert Jewish ancestry."

Abraham D. Lavender, Ph.D. Department of Sociology and Anthropology Florida International University, Miami, Florida.
From his book, "Searching For Crypto-Jews in France: From Spanish Jews to French Huguenots".

Chapter Six
Groups That Meet In Secret and Secret Groups

I found some historical similarities that are oceans apart but let me see if I cannot make a connection or at the very least, get us all *thinking*. I had ancestors that were in Leeuwarden back in the Middle Ages who I suspect were Jews posing as Christians. Leeuwarden is in Friesland, in very Northern Holland. Their history tells us that the French in 1818 decided that the "weapon of Leeuwarden" should be "blue with a climbing Lion of gold, the shield covered with a crown." The website where I read this information is: http://tuupovaarankoulu.jns.fi/comenius/hollanti/k ulttuurisivu/cultlw.html. Unfortunately, when I tried to return a couple of years later, the URL was not found on my server but here is the quote:

> "The name Leeuwarden has something to do with the Saint Vitus Cultus. The Dutch word "Leeuw" in Leeuwarden means Lion. We believe that Saint Vitus was thrown to the Lions in the Middle ages by emperor Diocletianus. Saint Vitus made a cross-sign with his hands and instead of eating him, the lions started to lick his feet. After several attempts to kill Saint Vitus finally the emperor succeeded killing Saint Vitus by burning him in a oven. Afterwards Saint Vitus became a Saint and the people worshipped him as a Guardian angel of the cities and villages."

The lion is obvious and I must say the reference to Saint Vitus burning in an oven startled me, especially at a time when I was researching the Inquisition and Crypto Jews.

While researching Saint Vitus, I ran across the history of E Clampus Vitus. The organization's history is rather cryptic. It began in Lewisport, Virginia. (Remember I'm researching Leeuwarden and Saint Vitus Cultus, and my trail leads me quickly to Lewisport and E Clampus Vitus.) Remember, Leeuwarden means "Lion Dwelling Hill" and one could argue that Lewisport means "Lions Port". The man who started E Clampus Vitus was Ephraim Bee. *Remember that name, Ephraim Bee*.

The man who commissioned Ephraim Bee to continue the Ancient and Honorable Order of E Clampus Vitus was "Caleb Cushing", the American minister to China. Caleb's name caught my eye as I had seen a posting on an ancestry message board where someone's ancestor had changed his surname to Cushing as "Cushnan sounded Jewish and he could not get a job".

E Clampus Vitas
(Latin) clampus
clam: secretly, in secret
vita: life, way of life

Before you put the book down, convinced that this author has indeed been listening to too much late night radio, read the genealogical information listed under the family files for the surname "Bee" and remember the man who began E Clampus Vitus was Ephraim Bee:

"The Bee Surname may have come from the French, LaBee (The Bee) It may have indicated that the person was a Bee Keeper or a quick swordsman... Another account is that they were descendants of the MaccaBees who fought to protect the Holy Land. The Surname later appears in The British Isles and from there into the Americas. It is said that when this family of "Bee" came from England to America, they had with them, the family record tracing their Jewish ancestry back through the tribe of Ephraim to Abraham. They had converted to Christianity but kept the true Sabbath and many became Seventh Day Baptists. The well-preserved family history was burned in a fire in New Jersey."

Before you say, "so what", remember the title of this book is *Secret Genealogy* and this chapter is *Secret Groups*.

According to the genealogist who has placed the family tree on familytreemaker at genealogy.com, the Ephraim Bee who started E. Clampus Vitus also designed the state seal for the state of West Virginia. Remember earlier when I stated that the French gave Leeuwarden the colors of blue and gold? What a fun coincidence that West Virginia's Legislature adopted "Old gold and blue" as the official state colors on March 5, 1963.

E Clampus Vitus took hold in California's gold country and the organization still exists today. I suggest reading their colorful Wikipedia history. Some members of E. Clampus Vitus were also members of the Masonic Lodge, one of the secret groups that keep coming up regarding Jews.

Secret Societies are fascinating. Conspiracy theorists love the challenge of trying to figure them out. You will be amused if you go on a tour of any of the groups' headquarters. A couple years ago, I toured the *Oddfellow's Hall* in a very small town. While walking upon the old, creaky wooden floors and gazing at the decades-old clothes on display behind glass cabinets, complete with helmets and swords, I had to wonder ... *who were these guys and what were they up to?* The Masons and the

Oddfellows will all quickly tell you that they are "A service group that helps the community". They also help one another and they make no secret about that. They have an ancient brotherhood parallel to the bond that ancient Jews had.

There are many legends regarding the beginning of the Oddfellows but one account I read said that their legend began in 1066, but they trace their origins "*back to the exile of the Israelites from Babylon in 587 B.C.*" The legend states that these exiled Israelites banded together into a "*brotherhood of mutual support and defense.*" The story continues with the fall of Jerusalem in AD 70 when, "*Israelites were taken to Rome by the Emperor Nero. Many of these captives subsequently served in the Roman army of Titus Caesar, who gave official recognition to their fraternity with a plate of gold with the emperor's dispensation engraved upon it.*"

www.ioofbc.org/subsidiary/History_in_Britain.pdf –

The popularity of this fraternity of soldiers within the Roman army spread "widely". In 100 A.D. an Oddfellow's lodge began in Britain. In 1000, the Roman soldiers also took it to Spain, then Portugal and France. Jean de Neuville and five French knights established a "Grand Lodge of Honour" in London in the 1100s. *Are these Jews who kept their brotherhood intact through centuries of war?*

How true the legend of the Oddfellow's is, I do not know but it is an accepted legend by many of the Order, at least according to this Oddfellow's website. They also state "similar fraternities did exist from classical times and did inherit many ideas from the eastern part of the Roman Empire – including Palestine and Babylon." In the 4th century, when it was *required* to be a Christian, the fraternities had to "Christianize". Sounds very similar to the "Crypto Jews" and the double lives they were forced into. Early European trade guilds adopted the style of these Middle Eastern type brotherhood fraternities. The Normans are said to have brought this style of guild to Britain.

The Jews may have formed fraternities early on, but by the time Christianity came along in Europe, many fraternities morphed into "trade guilds", which Jews were then excluded from, which is why many Jews have become proficient in occupations like banking and finance. However, a *secret society*, like the Order of Masons could have been a way for them to belong to a fraternity, especially if other Jews were already enmeshed into them for centuries. You can make a long list of similarities between some ancient Hebrew rituals and Masonic rituals. It's an interesting topic, especially when the beginning of Masonry is associated with the Knights Templar, attributed to creating the world's first banking system. The Knights Templar also began in Jerusalem when they occupied King Solomon's Temple. The Mason's headquarters in London has huge murals on the walls containing menorahs and other Jewish and Middle Eastern icons. If you are ever in London, make a visit to the Masonic Grand Lodge.

I must admit that the lure of the mystique behind secret societies interests me. But, since so many Jews were presenting themselves as Catholics, Huguenots, Walloons or other Protestant denominations, we can't begin to know when history shows Jews joining Masonic groups. The thought that Jews hide amongst the secret society of Masons is intriguing to me because my maternal and paternal grandmothers were each in the female branch of the Masons, *Eastern Star* for over fifty years. It is a requirement that a woman be admitted through a Mason, typically a father or brother so obviously my grandmothers had ties. You can do some research on your own and see what others write about the secret society of the

Masons. The websites of their detractors provide plenty of information. However, is it true?

I can imagine how Masonry could be Jewish worship gone "underground" so to speak but I have come to believe that the organization has taken on an identity of its own. It may have acquired its main template of worship from the early Hebrew practices of worship but if you think about it so did Catholicism and the Protestant religions as well and look how they've changed through the centuries. Let's not forget that the Jews *were* the first to come up with monotheism.

I am under the impression that it is a lot more exciting to be a conspiracy theorist investigating the Masons, than it is to be a Mason. Every Mason I've ever met came across as a normal businessman and business can get pretty dull. Their London headquarters is a nice tourist spot. When I took the tour, the tour guide pointed out a middle-aged man in a suit and introduced him as a "modern day Mason". He had appeared to be on the tour but I wonder if he wasn't just keeping tabs on the tour guide. After the tour, I was with my family out in front of the building. He could see we were baffled. He walked up to me and said something to the effect of, "You want to know what this is all about?" and he laughed and tossed a small packet of Starbucks sugar into my hand. (See pages 52 & 76).

So what do people do when they are not *accepted* by a Rabbi because they aren't Jewish, yet they *feel Jewish* because their families have been practicing Judaism, in their own way, for centuries? There are many groups someone may join and some of the people in these groups are *very secretive.*

There is a Crypto-Jewish movement underway, particularly in the southwestern United States. The Internet is full of websites and interesting stories regarding modern day descendants of history's hidden Jews. Judaism requires conversion from non-Jews and present day Rabbis are strict about it. Some of today's Crypto-Jews complain about being "left out", which is why many of the Crypto-Jews have chosen to create their own "Jewish" group. There is an Association of Crypto Jews, for Hispanic Sephardim. Even if you are not interested in joining, it's interesting to see the pictures they have posted. From the smiles on their faces, you can see they enjoy worshipping the religion of their ancient ancestors. You will find them at www.cryptojew.org.

"Throughout its stormy history, from the Roman period until the present, Jews have lived in France, their fate intimately tied to the various kings and leaders. Despite physical hardship and anti-Semitism, Jewish intellectual and spiritual life flourished, producing some of the most famous Jewish rabbis and thinkers, including Rashi and Rabenu Tam. Jews have contributed to all aspects of French culture and society and have excelled in finance, medicine, theater and literature. Currently, France hosts Europe's largest Jewish community and Paris is said to have more kosher restaurants than even New York City."

http://www.jewishvirtuallibrary.org/jsource/vjw/France.html

Chapter Seven
My Ancestry ... Are We Related?

Even if you are no relation to me, the information in this chapter is informative. My family tree is large and holds the names of many prominent North American surnames whose connecting family trees hold thousands of members. I suggest you at least scan this chapter, as some points may have bearing on *your* family tree. While you go through this chapter, keep in mind that several years ago when I began to deeply research my family tree, I had no idea that my ancestors were Jewish. I hadn't a clue. I used to assume that my ancestors had always been Christians. The men in my mother's tree were recorded as having been ministers and deacons and the women taught Sunday school and brought flowers for the alter on Sunday and holidays. And as far as my father's family goes, my mother used to say, *"They were all preachers"*.

In the early stages of my researching, I started collecting so many names with whom my ancestors colonized with, married, bought from, sold to, etc. that I started calling them "the gang" and found it crucial that I research their names too. The clues that lay in the names of the associates were dead-giveaways. During the Diaspora Jews stuck together, and after all these years, during Colonial times, these pioneer American families were still sticking together. I often wonder whether the younger generations were aware of their Jewish heritage or if the older generations guided them to choose Jewish partners. A sort of silent conspiracy between sets of Jewish parents may have existed. Heated arguments must have ensued over whether or not to completely abandon Jewish origins which would enable new generations freedom from persecution and access to advantages in the New World or to hang on desperately to the last vestiges of their ancient bonds.

One French ancestor of mine is "David des Marets". David is a Jewish name and Marets sounds and looks like "Marais" (swamp), the name of the old Jewish Quarter on the Left Bank in Paris. His name could literally mean *David of the Swamp*. This could also *not* be the truth of his surname but when you put all the names together that your ancestors associated with in business and the names of the families these ancestors allowed their sons and daughters to marry, like pieces of a puzzle, you begin to see the picture and they begin to come alive. Then you find another surname in the family, like "Heubeck". It is not exclusively a Jewish name but plenty of Jews have the surname Huebeck. If you are fortunate enough to have the time, the patience and a few names, you too can bring your ancestors to life.

American first names were commonly *Anglicized*. Names like Antjn became Ann, Magdalena became Lena, etc. So we must investigate first names as well because even though Mary may sound English it may derive from Maria and before that Miryam which is Hebrew.

Eventually, I ran across the name of the oldest ancestor (he was born in 1569) I know of, "Epke Lieuwesz". (Other spellings I've seen are Epcke Luvesc, Lieuwes and Luuesz). I had been looking at names on Sephardim.com. It fit, as did others.

"In some cases the awareness of a Jewish heritage was passed from generation to generation. Children were told about it when whey reached teenage years. Much of their Jewish knowledge was lost in the ensuing 350 years, however many families maintained certain rituals which indicated a Jewish background: They lit candies on Friday nights; They slaughtered animals in a kosher way; They read only the "Old Testament"; They shunned pork and shellfish; They refrained from eating bread in the week before Easter; They would not cook meat in its own blood."
http://www.saudades.org/cryptobraz.html

Of course that is not proof that an ancestor was of Jewish origins but I had enough suspicions to keep going. I had huge doubts as well but time after time, there would explode onto the page another clue, another piece of that puzzle. It was exciting. They were speaking to me from the grave. I had my own Da Vinci Code type conspiracy and it was mine to unravel.

My ancestors had a hard time deciding whether they would go by, Leeuw, Jacobs, Epke, Bonte, Bonta or any numerous variations of those names. Historically, in the Torah/Bible the name "Jacob" began as "Yakoov". It comes from the Hebrew word "akev", which means "heel". Jacob is a very popular Jewish surname.

In Holland in 1640, the descendant of my oldest ancestral line begins to sign his name as "Jacobi Epkes te Bonta". The name "Leeuw" (Dutch for lion) has been dropped. I could do a whole chapter on the variations of the Lion surname: Lewis, Luis, Luiz, Lyon, Leao, Loewe, Luvesc, etc. Eventually "Jacobi" was also dropped and today the surname lives on as "Banta". I found an interesting legal brief on the Internet stating that the son of Jean Rothschild who changed his surname to "Bonta" had been awarded money from a Swiss bank account that had been lost to the Nazis. I've seen it mentioned that "Bento" stems from "Baruch" which *means blessed in Hebrew.* World-famous medieval Jewish philosopher, Baruch Spinoza's original Portuguese name was "Bento de

Espinosa". Today the surname Banta is seen all around the world. I looked at the phonebook pages for Israeli names and there were plenty of Bantas.

Family records reveal the "Leeuw" family lived for a while at Aram, Friesland. What is the true origin of the name of this community? In a google.com search, I found this entry in "The International Standard Bible Encyclopedia", by Geoffrey W. Bromiley:

"A letter written by the Jews of Elephantine (408 BC) speaks of frankincense (Aram, l'bonta) as an element of the temple cult, alongside whole offerings and..."

I was just trying to find a little history for the ancient village of "Aram" in the Netherlands. The definition of Aramaean/Aramean is, "One of a large Semitic group occupying the Biblical Aram (in the middle Euphrates Valley) and neighboring territories. The tongue spoken by Jesus was Aramaic."

A coincidence? You just have to shake your head. Who were these people and what were their origins?

Epke Jacobse (Banta) is listed in the *History of New York* as being "The earliest ancestor of the Banta family in America". On February 12th, 1659,

Epke Jacobse (Banta) immigrated from Minnertsga, Friesland, The Netherlands, on the ship "de Trouw". "De Trouw" means "The Faith". Epke traveled with his wife, Sitske Dircksda and his five children. The oldest was six-years-old, the youngest was only nine-months-old.

The names of some of the women in my family, Sitske and Sil, sound Eastern European, Polish maybe, while a name like Epcke Luvesc sounds Portuguese. However, during this early era, the Middle Ages, the names in my family tree sound like a European mix.

When one sees odd names like, "Reytske Sickedr" one remembers you are dealing with *foreigners*. I didn't get far researching "Reytske" but I did find a Jewish woman with the last name of "Retske". Sounds the same but what does it all mean? Further search reveals a village named Retske near Kurenets in Belarus, an area that figures prominently in Jewish history.

Another female ancestor during the Middle Ages had the name "Sitske Trietske Dirchsda". I did find some clues to ponder. Trijntje is the Dutch form of Katrijn. Sitske sounds a lot like a man's Yiddish name "Chatzkel" but the "ke" on the end of "Sitske" is a nickname kind of thing. Her "real name would be "Sits" (Sitz) meaning "victory", which is used by both Germans and Jews, about right if she lived in Holland.

On the website sephardim.com they will list a name that is used, though not always exclusively, by Sephardic Jews. Then they place a number next to it as a reference for the resource where they found it. I have listed some of the names in my family tree that are listed in sephardim.com. and have italicized them. After the names, I present the equivalent found at sephardim.com.

(The italicized surnames are in my family tree.)
Dircksda, "Dirckson" was an alias used for the true Sephardic name of "Baruch".
Bric (*Brickers*)
de *Leeuw*, an alias used for the true Sephardic name of "de Leon".
(Luis and Luiz are also listed as Sephardic names).
Jacobs, Jacobi
Cornel, *Cornelisdr* (The "dr" means "daughter of" in Zeeland, "se", "sen" or "szen" mean "son of")
Camara, Camayor, *Cammerer / Kammerer*
Marash, Marte, Marti, de Mera, de Mora, de Marinas, *des Marets*,
Rotenberg, Rotin, Rote, *Roten, Wroten*
Scha, Schuhami, *Shuck*
Seba, *Seba*
Sicsu, *Sickedr*
Fonte, *Fonda*

Morris, Morrais, Moris, Morro, Moro, Moros, Morrow

Another set of ancestors is "Andrew and Margaret Shuck". "Shuk" is definitely a Jewish name for someone from Shuki Lithuania. "Schuh" can be German, also spelled as "Schuck". I have also seen the mention of a "Rabbi" Shuck.

No doubt Muslims and Jews fell in love and intermarried, especially during the Middle Ages when in Spain the Arabs and Jews shared their love of exploring science, math, philosophy, religion, architecture and life's deep questions. When you look at lists of Jewish surnames, you will see names with possible Arabic origins. I've seen it mentioned that the surname "Alfon" might have originated with the Spanish Moors because of the name beginning with Al. In addition, as I mentioned earlier in the book, I have also wondered about the surname "Moore" and it's variations of "Morris", "Morse", etc. Sometimes we think of "Morris" as Scots-Irish but it's fun to dig deeper. It also makes me want to look toward the Middle East for the origins of Morris Dancing, an ancient dance popular throughout the British Isles. No one seems to know where the dance originated. The dance remains alive and well. In recent years, it has been performed around the infamous Maypole that Englishman, John Winthrop of Colonial America was so chastised for celebrating during the Pagan celebration of Beltane.

Amidst these Dutch-sounding names on my family tree is the surname "Fonda". Had I just accepted that the surname was Dutch, I would have never discovered an ancestry message board posting that said that *during the Inquisition*, "the family was reported and they fled Spain to Genoa, Italy." What a great day that was for me. I now need to study the names in this person's family tree and see if it doesn't match up with any of my names. I guess the family "only stayed in Italy long enough to assume Italian identity and then went on to Holland where many Spaniards had taken refuge."

Another great day of researching was when I read a story about someone visiting Friesland and going to the old homestead where my ancient ancestors lived back in the Middle Ages. The earliest name I have for this ancestor is "Leeuw", *the Dutch word for Lion*. The site of the Leeuw homestead was still visible and another homestead, not related but historically associated with the family held "two great stone lions at the entrance".

Remember that many Jews, forced to leave Spain, had already converted to Christianity. We don't know what our ancestors had to endure; we may have done the same thing. But first they were

Jews and then they weren't and then they were again ... I guess it depended on how safe they and their families were. And of course, there were Jews who *became Christians of their own accord*.

I love to really dig away at surnames. One name was especially fun for me - I don't know how accurate I am but let me show you where I went with it. I have an ancestor by the name of "Jan Albertsen Ter Hunen". The family eventually became "Terhune". Family researchers also claim it was originally "ter Hune". Hune is a Jewish first name. I googled "La Hune" and found that Newfoundland has a cape by that name, ok, so what? But more importantly, there appears to be a neighborhood in Paris's Left Bank called La Hune. Paris's Left Bank may figure prominently in your genealogical search if your ancestors were "French" (or Jews who went to France from Spain or Portugal). Wealthy Sephardic Jews built communities on the Left Bank of the Seine River. The name for the old Jewish quarter, located on the Left Bank is "Le Marais", which means the swamp. If you have "French" ancestry with surnames that sound similar to this, as in Des Marets, Maretz, etc. you should consider that they might have been Jews.

Old English is the period between about 450-1100. It is during this historical period that "har hune" meant downy plant or the common name for

Horehound, which is *the bitter herb used for Passover*. I have several Jewish clues here. One, a neighborhood in Paris's Left Bank where an ancient Jewish Quarter began. Two, I have Hune as a Jewish first name, and three, it's the Old English word for the bitter herb used for Passover.

These three things prove nothing and one could wonder if I don't have better things to do with my time but here's where it gets interesting. I researched the word "ter" and it is a Portuguese word that means, have, got, hold, to possess or have in ones hands. So that means Ter Hune could very well mean to *possess the bitter herb for Passover*. In addition, the Diaspora could have taken them through Portugal. (Though for the Dutch, "ter" means "to" or "at"). On a genealogical message board, I found where a Terhune mentions several first names, "David, Ruth and Goldie," all popular Jewish names.

Prepositions that are used for Portuguese surnames are "da", "das," "do", "dos", and "de". And in Portuguese, most but not all names that end in es are patronymic. When one immigrates to a new country one alters their name to fit into the new country. Our ancestors had no idea that their choices would one day frustrate genealogists.

"Before the Lower East Side of New York, before the Marais district in Paris, even before London's Park Lane, there was Vlooienburg. They spoke to one another in Portuguese and read classic works of Spanish literature to their children. They might also have known some Hebrew. But these were, according to official documents, 'Portuguese merchants', and at least in the eyes of the municipal authorities, Christians. Or so everyone pretended."

Steven Nadler, "Rembrandt's Jews", University of Chicago Press

In 1640, my ancestor, Epke te Bonte resided in Friesland, in the Netherlands. You would think he was a rock star by the number of websites he's mentioned on. The only Epke more famous is a famous gymnast named Epke. Other than these two men, millenniums apart, the name is not common. Even before Napoleon required the Dutch to come up with surnames (Epke had immigrated to the colony of New Amsterdam by then) the family had a hard time deciding what they would call themselves. It appears that the name "Bonte" came from the name of the family farm that was near Arum, Friesland. Where they came up with that name is unknown but in Chapter Four I discussed the "Bani-Israel" which means, *Children of Israel*.

It also appears that by 1656 one of the Bonte clan could not decide what religion to be. Epke's son Epke was arrested, fined and required to appear before the public prosecutor *because he permitted a Roman Catholic priest into his home to baptize his child*. That also drew my attention early in my ancestral search. I had read that *Jews made a big show of their Christianity* through a variety of ways. The subsequent family history shows that he was a member of the Dutch Reformed Church, so ... go figure.

There is a discussion going on at one of the ancestry message boards about the surname

"Cornejo". I have enjoyed reading the posts because my female ancestor, "Sil Corndeliz" is a mystery. Because the name "Cornejo" means dogwood tree in Spanish, some believe that it's a Jewish surname that arose during the Inquisition when Jews were forced to convert and often gave themselves names from nature. But take it apart and it is "Corn de Liz" or "Corn of Lizbon". Even today Lisbon, Portugal is spelled by some as *Lizbon*.

Claims on Cornejo ancestry message boards state connections to Spanish "Knights of Saint James". Another states, "There was a Duke who built a cathedral near Granada, Spain". Someone else claims the name "Cornejo" means "son of Cornelius" and has its origins among the old Romans. Though it sounds so very English, it is known to have begun in Britain only toward the end of the fourteenth century. The name "Cornelius" has become a common first name but if you say it slowly, it sounds very much like "Corndeliz".

Since I am always on the lookout for any Jewish connection to Corndeliz, I took note when I saw another posting that mentioned "Jan Cornelisse Groen" (1662). "Groen" was the second most common Jewish name in Europe. The community he came from, Oud Beijerland, south of Rotterdam, also has a Jewish community. What

I derive from this is that though "Corndeliz" doesn't sound Jewish, it could be. Korn is Yiddish for "grain", which would probably make it an Ashkenazic surname. "Korner" is Middle/High German for "miller" or perhaps the manager of a granary. The roots of "Corn" are worth researching further. Add up your own clues. Were your Jewish ancestors Sephardic nature lovers or Ashkenazi grain peddlers?

In the year 1000 in the Rhine Valley, near Worms and Mainz, there was a Rabbi training school. European Jews gravitated to the area. By the Middle Ages, the Jews in Europe contributed to the new accelerated growth of knowledge that sprang from the area. They brought the Talmud from the Holy Land, indulged in lively philosophical discussions, and developed strong friendships with Christian theologians. If you read Jewish history you'll understand how intellectually active Jews were in the Netherlands, Belgium and Germany during the Middle Ages.

Sometimes it doesn't take long to find that an ancestor was Jewish, maybe just years and not decades. Kidding aside, once you know what to look for you could uncover a lot in an afternoon. You may get a few surprises. Everyone has a famous relation. Rarely does one not get excited and or brag about a famous relative. We all have some, if you do not you just have not spent enough time doing genealogy.

I try to uncover all the Jewish clues in my family tree. Alone, most of them mean nothing but pieced together it forms a mosaic of lovers and farmers, religious hoppers, fighters, mothers and fathers, adventurers, weavers and potters, writers, politicians, revolutionaries, stubborn fools and debutants, etc. I write novels about them. These were real people. I love these people.

Chapter Eight
Interesting Websites

An excellent resource for searching Sephardic surnames:
www.sephardim.com

An Index to the Given Names in the 1292 Census of   Paris:
http://heraldry.sca.org/laurel/names/paris.html

University of Notre Dame Latin Dictionary and Grammar Aid:
http://archives.nd.edu/latgramm.htm

This is the list of names of the Portuguese Sephardim who were paid to leave Amsterdam during the years 1757 – 1813:
http://www.saudades.org/leaveamsterdam.html

Notarial Records from Amsterdam's Portuguese Jewish Community that Mention Danzig:
http://www.jewishgen.org/Danzig/amsterdam.php

Shira Schoenberg's Virtual Jewish History Tour of England:
http://www.jewishvirtuallibrary.org/jsource/vjw/England.html

This is an excellent website for researching Dutch History:

http://www.rabbel.nl/oldplaces1.html

Two websites for researching Dutch Jewry:
http://www.nljewgen.org/eng/index.html
http://www.dutchjewry.org/

Sephardic Surnames from a number of Jewish Sephardic sources:
http://www.sephardicgen.com/names.htm

Search for ancestors among free lists and records:
http://www.olivetreegenealogy.com/nn/

Cyndi's List of Genealogy Sites on the Internet:
http://www.cyndislist.com
http://www.CyndisList.com/jewish.htm

Istanbul Jewish Genealogy Project (almost 100,000 records):
http://www.benkazez.com/dan/istanbul/

Definitions of the world's major religions and belief systems:
http://www.cftech.com/BrainBank/OTHERREFERENCE/RELIGION/MajorReligion.html

Avotaynu: Resources for tracing Jewish Family History:
www.avotaynu.com/nu.htm

For a study on hypocorism (a naming pattern):

http://en.wikipedia.org/wiki/Hypocorism

Jewish Names and Naming Patterns:
https://wiki.familysearch.org/en/Jewish_Names_Pe
rsonal

A List of Jewish Surnames, History and Origin:
http://humora.tripod.com/Surnames.html

Southern Appalachian / Melungeon Heritage:
http://www.melungeon.org/

An interesting discussion about similarities
between Cajuns and Jews:
http://www.freerepublic.com/focus/f-
news/1337161/replies?c=25

Behind the Name/the etymology and history of
first names:
www.behindthename.com

Grand Lodge of British Columbia Independent
Order of Odd Fellows:
http://www.ioofbc.org/index.htm

History of the Oddfellows:
http://www.oddfellows.org.uk/History.htm

The History of The Ancient and Honorable Order
of E Clampus Vitus:
http://en.wikipedia.org/wiki/E_Clampus_Vitus

An Interesting and Historically Informative Article Regarding Maranos:
http://www.jewishencyclopedia.com/view.jsp?arti d=169&letter=M

The Association of Crypto Jews:
http://www.cryptojew.org/main_page.html

A short history of the famous scholar and orator, Menasseh Ben Israel, beloved by both Jews and Gentiles: http://www.saudades.org/menasseh.html

The Twelve Tribes of Israel Engraved Upon Stone:
http://www.templesanjose.org/JudaismInfo/history /12tribes.htm

GLOSSARY

<u>Acadia</u> – original French name of Nova Scotia

<u>Acadian</u> – from Acadia

<u>Akkad</u> – (Accad) the northern division of ancient Babylonia

<u>Akkadian</u> – one of the Semitic people of Mesopotamia before 2000 B.C.E.

<u>Anglicize</u> – to translate, reword or express into English usage

<u>Anglo-Saxon</u> – a member of the nation created by the merger of Germanic tribes who invaded England and resided from the fifth to the eleventh centuries; person of English descent consisting of mixed races; "Old English"

<u>Anusim</u> - an ancient Hebrew word meaning "people who have been forced"

<u>Arab</u> – member of a Semitic race from the Arabian Peninsula and North Africa

<u>Ashkenazi</u> – noun for a Yiddish-speaking Jew from Middle, Northern and Eastern Europe (Ashkenazim is plural whereas Ashkenazic is used as the adjective)

<u>Auto de Fe</u> - the Inquisitional ceremony that pronounced the judgment of execution, which usually meant burning heretics to death

<u>Bible</u> – sacred book of Christians (Old & New Testaments); sacred book of Judaism (Old Testament), referred to as the Torah

<u>Black Dutch</u> – a term sometimes used by Native Americans to conceal their ethnicity (also Black

143

Irish); a term sometimes used by the Dutch for the Spanish Jews who immigrated to the Netherlands in the 16th century; a term sometimes used by German Jews to conceal their ethnicity

Cajun – person of Acadian descent

Calque – used in Jewish naming patterns, the process of taking a word from the local language that's similar to the sacred name and using it for a name (a translation)

Christian – believer in Christianity; member of a Christian church; person whose life and character conform to Christ's teachings

Christianize – to make Christian; to convert to Christianity

Christian name – first name, given to Christians at baptism

Converso – a Jew who converted to Christianity, usually by force or coercion

Court Jews (Hofjude) - Jews attaining powerful positions in European aristocracy as bankers, money managers, consultants, trade and political representatives, etc.

Crypto Jew – practicing Judaism in secret while professing another religious faith

Diaspora – Jews scattered throughout the ancient world after Exile

Emigrate – to leave a country or region to settle in another

Eponym – historical or legendary person from whom a family, nation, race, etc. takes its name

Hasidim – meaning "the pious", a Jewish religious movement that began in the 1700s, focusing on the emotions and sentiments of faith rather than dogma and ritual

Hassidic - of or relating to the Jewish Hasidim or its members or their beliefs and practices

Hebrew – member of one of the Semitic peoples inhabiting ancient Palestine; language of the Hebrews; also a book in the New Testament of the Bible

Heretic – one who holds an opinion contrary to Christian belief and encourages separation from the church

Huguenot – a French Protestant during the 16th & 17th centuries (Walloon refers to Belgian Protestants)

Hypocorism – a hypocorism is the lesser form of a given name used in more intimate situations, like a nickname, originating from the Greek expression to "use child talk"

Immigrate - to come into a country as a permanent resident

Indentured Servants – apprentice bound to a master by a contract, or to service in a colony etc.

Inquisition – the establishment of the Holy Office (tribunal) used to pursue and punish heretics

Israel – used to describe: the northern Hebrew kingdom, the descendants of Jacob (Jews) and/or the republic in SW Asia along the Mediterranean

Jew – a member of the ancient tribe of Judah, also, one who practices the religion of Judaism, a Hebrew

Jewish – pertinent to or like the Jews

Judah – son of Jacob and Leah, also; one of the twelve tribes of Israel, also; the Hebrew kingdom in Southern Palestine

Judea – the southern area of ancient Palestine that formed the kingdom of the tribes of Judah and Benjamin

Hebraic - of or pertaining to the Hebrews or to the Hebrew kingdom in Southern Palestine

Judaism – religion, culture and ethos of the Jews

Kinnui – (kinouy, kinui) not a sacred Jewish name but a name that relates to the immediate environment, a secular name required at circumcision along with the sacred name

Kosher – (kasher) from the Hebrew word meaning "fit" or "proper", usually used to define food that has been ritually cleaned according to Jewish law

Ladino – the mixed Spanish and Hebrew language spoken by Sephardim

Law of the Pure Blood – a prohibition against migrating to Mexico unless one could prove that the last three generations of their family had been "Old Christians"

Marrano – taken from the Spanish word "swine", it was used for Jews who professed Christianity only to escape death or persecution during the Inquisition, while often continuing to observe Judaism secretly. It is believed the term came about when Jews broke kosher dietary laws and put pork in their food to prove they no longer practiced Judaism

Matronymic – name derived from that of the mother

Medieval – of or pertaining to the Middle Ages

Melungeon – a group of people descended from European and Middle Eastern ancestry who intermarried with Native Americans and African Americans and reside along North America's Atlantic coast, including northeastern Tennessee and southwestern Virginia

Mexican Inquisition – an extension of the Spanish Inquisition into the New World

Moor – native of Morocco or North African states; a Moslem or Arab who settled in North Africa; a descendant of the Saracens who invaded Spain during the Middle Ages

Morisco – a Moor, especially of Spain

Mulatto – person with a light-browned skin pigmentation of mixed African and Caucasian ancestry

New Christian – Jews or Moors who converted or were forced to convert to Christianity during the Middle Age's Inquisitional period of history

Patronymic – name derived from that of the father

Pureza de la sangre – "purity of the blood" certificate needed during the Mexican Inquisition to avoid arrest

Rabbi – spiritual leader of a Jewish synagogue; a Jewish teacher or doctor of the law

<u>Samaria</u> – ancient region of Palestine

<u>Schem Hakodesch</u> – sacred Hebrew name required at circumcision, the name is used in Hebrew documents and in the synagogue

<u>Semite</u> – a descendant of Shem (a son of Noah); a member of a Caucasian race now chiefly represented by the Jews and Arabs, but in ancient times included the Phoenicians, Assyrians, Babylonians, Aramaeans, etc

<u>Semitic</u> – of or pertinent to the Semites

<u>Sephardim</u> – descendants of the former Jews of Spain and Portugal (Sephardim is the noun, Sephardic is the adjective)

<u>Slave</u> – a person held in bondage

<u>Synagogue –</u> Jewish house of worship

<u>Torah</u> – entire body of Jewish law, the *Pentateuch,* which is the first five books of the Old Testament of the Bible

<u>Walloon</u> – a term used to refer to Belgian Protestants, while the term "Huguenot" denotes French back-ground

<u>Yiddish</u> – a High German dialect developed under Hebrew and Slavic influence, written in Hebrew letters

<u>Voorleser</u> – the Dutch word for an educated man who read lessons in church (absent a pastor) led singing, taught school and performed other duties

BIBLIOGRAPHY

A Frisian Family, The Banta Genealogy, by Theodore
Banta, 1893.

A Huguenot on the Hackensack: David Demarest and His Legacy by David C. Major, Fairleigh Dickinson University Press, 2007.

ancestry.com

A PEOPLE'S HISTORY OF THE UNITED STATES, 1492 – PRESENT by Howard Zinn, HarperCollins Publishers Inc., NY, NY, 2003.

Atlas of the Year 1000 by John Man, Harvard University Press, Cambridge, Massachusetts, 1999.

BANTA Pioneers and Records of The Wives and Allied Families, by Elsa M. Banta, 1983.

Cultural Atlas of the World, THE JEWISH WORLD by Nicholas de Lange, Andromeda Oxford Ltd, 1988.

genealogy.com

HERITAGE, CIVILIZATION and the JEWS by Abba Eban, Summit Books-SIMON & SCHUSTER, NEW YORK, NY 10020, 1984.

History of the Oddfellows
www.ioofbc.org/subsidiary/History_in_Britain.pdf
-
http://www.familytreedna.com/public/NuevoMexico/

http://www.4crests.com/cornejo-coat-of-arms.html

http://www.jewishvirtuallibrary.org/jsource/US-Israel/amsterdam.html

http://en.wikipedia.org/wiki/Leeuwarden

Internet Jewish History Sourcebook
http://www.fordham.edu/halsall/jewish/jewishsbook.html

Jewish Genealogical Society of Bergen County

Jewish message board at Ancestry.com

Jewish mess board at genealogy.com

Longoria, Frank
http://www.star-telegram.com/homes/longoria/

Mazornet, Inc. "Dedicated to compile helpful information and resources concerning Jewish Genetic Diseases."
www.mazornet.com

Rembrandt's Jews, by Steven Nadler, The
University of Chicago Press, Chicago, 2003.

SEARCHING FOR CRYPTO-JEWS IN
FRANCE: FROM SPANISH JEWS TO FRENCH
HUGUENOTS, by Abraham D. Lavender, Ph.D.
Department of Sociology and Anthropology
Florida International University, Miami, Florida
from HaLapid, December 1996.

THE AMERICAN HERITAGE HISTORY OF
THE THIRTEEN COLONIES, by the Editors of
American Heritage, American Heritage Publishing
Co. Inc., USA, 1967.

THE GIFTS OF THE JEWS, How a Tribe of
Desert Nomads Changed the Way Everyone
Thinks and Feels, by Thomas Cahill, Nan A.
Talese, Bantam Doubleday Dell, NY 1998.

THE HOLY BIBLE, ENCYCLOPEDIC INDEX,
CONCORDANCE AND DICTIONARY,
CONSOLIDATED BOOK PUBLISHERS,
CHICAGO, ILLINOIS, 1956.

The International Standard Bible Encyclopedia, by
Geoffrey W. Bromiley, 1995.

151

The Jewish Mama's Kitchen, by Denise Phillips, Thunder Bay Press, MQ Publications Limited, 2005.

The presence of Africans in Elizabethan England (www.thefreelibrary.com)

The Scribner-Bantam English Dictionary, Bantam Books, NY, NY, 1980.

The Sikh-Jewish Coalition http://sikhandjewshallfind.blogspot.com/2008/02/blog-post_07.html

The Slave Trade, by Hugh Thomas, Simon & Schuster, New York, NY, 1997.

The Spanish Cookbook, by Barbara Norman, Bantam, 1971, NY, NY.

Webster's Collegiate Dictionary, Fifth Edition, G. & C. Merriam Co., Publishers, Springfield, Mass., 1941.

www.sephardim.com

www.jewishencyclopedia.com

INDEX